the Food & Cooking of
Peru

the Food & Cooking of
Peru

TRADITIONS • INGREDIENTS • TASTES • TECHNIQUES • 65 CLASSIC RECIPES

Flor Arcaya de Deliot

aqua marine

This edition is published by Aquamarine, an imprint of Anness Publishing Ltd, Hermes House, 88–89 Blackfriars Road, London SE1 8HA; tel. 020 7401 2077; fax 020 7633 9499

www.aquamarinebooks.com; www.annesspublishing.com

If you like the images in this book and would like to investigate using them for publishing, promotions or advertising, please visit our website www.practicalpictures.com for more information.

UK agent: The Manning Partnership Ltd; tel. 01225 478444; fax 01225 478440; sales@manning-partnership.co.uk
UK distributor: Book Trade Services; tel. 0116 2759086; fax 0116 2759090; uksales@booktradeservices.com; exportsales@booktradeservices.com
North American agent/distributor: National Book Network; tel. 301 459 3366; fax 301 429 5746; www.nbnbooks.com
Australian agent/distributor: Pan Macmillan Australia; tel. 1300 135 113; fax 1300 135 103; customer.service@macmillan.com.au
New Zealand agent/distributor: David Bateman Ltd; tel. (09) 415 7664; fax (09) 415 8892

Publisher: Joanna Lorenz
Editorial Director: Helen Sudell
Executive Editor: Joanne Rippin
Designer: Adelle Morris
Photography: Jon Whitaker
Food Stylist: Fergal Connelly
Prop Stylist: Penny Markham
Production Controller: Wendy Lawson
Proofreading Manager: Lindsay Zamponi
Editorial Reader: Penelope Goodare

ETHICAL TRADING POLICY

Because of our ongoing ecological investment programme, you, as our customer, can have the pleasure and reassurance of knowing that a tree is being cultivated on your behalf to naturally replace the materials used to make the book you are holding. For further information about this scheme, go to www.annesspublishing.com/trees.

NOTES

Bracketed terms are intended for American readers.
For all recipes, quantities are given in both metric and imperial measures and, where appropriate, in standard cups and spoons. Follow one set of measures, but not a mixture, because they are not interchangeable.
Standard spoon and cup measures are level. 1 tsp = 5ml, 1 tbsp = 15ml, 1 cup = 250ml/8fl oz.
Australian standard tablespoons are 20ml. Australian readers should use 3 tsp in place of 1 tbsp for measuring small quantities.
American pints are 16fl oz/2 cups. American readers should use 20fl oz/2.5 cups in place of 1 pint when measuring liquids.
Electric oven temperatures in this book are for conventional ovens. When using a fan oven, the temperature will probably need to be reduced by about 10–20°C/20–40°F. Since ovens vary, you should check with your manufacturer's instruction book for guidance.
The nutritional analysis given for each recipe is calculated per portion (i.e. serving or item), unless otherwise stated. If the recipe gives a range, such as Serves 4–6, then the nutritional analysis will be for the smaller portion size, i.e. 6 servings.
Measurements for sodium do not include salt added to taste.
Medium (US large) eggs are used unless otherwise stated.

PUBLISHER'S NOTE

Although the advice and information in this book are believed to be accurate and true at the time of going to press, neither the authors nor the publisher can accept any legal responsibility or liability for any errors or omissions that may be made nor for any inaccuracies nor for any harm or injury that comes about from following instructions or advice in this book.

Contents

The culinary history of Peru

The fascinating history of Peru goes back many centuries, and there is good evidence that people were cultivating the land there more than 15,000 years ago. Archaeological finds such as the remnants of buildings, utensils and traces of irrigation ditches have established that basic agricultural and fishing techniques were flourishing in that period. Eventually, Peruvian society developed into the sophisticated empire of the Incas, which although subsequently overthrown by the Spanish, still has a profound influence on the cultural traditions of the country.

Early humans in Peru

The very earliest traces of farming have been found in the mountains and foothills of the Andes. These early settlers hunted for game, but soon learned to cultivate crops by saving and planting seed. This is the origin of Peru's wonderfully rich seed bank, giving so many varieties of basic plants such as potatoes and corn, but also fruits not found anywhere else. These early settlers also kept domesticated animals such as llamas. Those who settled near the sea spent their time fishing rather than cultivating the land, and learned to trade with the inland groups for a varied diet.

Below: Pachacutec, the king who expanded the Inca empire and built the city of Machu Picchu.

The rise of the Incas

From about the second millennium, Peru began to develop elaborate societies, which became the basis for the great Inca empire. These early groups built larger and larger settlements that grew into great cities but they also fought each other for dominance. Lambayeque, Chimu, Chincha, Chachapoyas, Chancay and other evocatively named cities mark the places where these great kingdoms began. The level of sophistication was high, as shown by the textiles and ceramics that have survived from this period.

In the 12th century, Inca civilization began to develop and grow in strength. Eventually, by 1450, the great leader Pachacutec oversaw

Above: This doorway from the ruined Inca city, Choquequirao, in the Cuzco region, shows the characteristic large stone blocks with which the Inca builders constructed their cities.

Above left: Llamas still graze around the ruins of Machu Picchu, the 'lost city' of the Incas, just as they did centuries ago.

Above: Francisco Pizarro, the leader of the Spanish conquistadors who arrived in Peru in 1530.

Below: The Inti Raymi 'Festival of the Sun' was a religious ceremony of the Inca Empire. A theatrical representation of the festival takes place on 24 June in Sacsayhuamán.

the spread of the Inca empire over the whole country and subdued all the smaller social groups. The Incas at their height had an empire of 11 million people, all of whom were organized and fed by a strict and carefully planned strategy of keeping the wealthy in check while taking care of the poor. Each harvest was used for the good of all, the weak and the strong, the farmers and the administrators, the peasants and the religious leaders alike.

The Inca people ate a varied diet, as their system of communications meant that there was a flourishing trade between all the corners of the empire. The Incas even had a most impressive system of delivery men known as 'chasquis', runners who joined up with each other in a relay system that meant fresh produce could be transported with ease. It is said that fresh fish from the coast could be eaten in Cusco, a city over 320km (200 miles) inland.

The main product was corn in all its forms: fresh, dry and toasted, and even as an alcoholic drink (chicha). But the Incas also ate many different vegetables and fruits, honey, freshwater fish, sea fish and shellfish, and meat products. The coca leaf was believed to be a sacred plant and was chewed as part of the Incas' religious rituals.

The Spanish conquest

Sadly for the Incas, they began to fall out among themselves, and a devastating civil war between two brothers left them open to easy conquest by the Spanish, who arrived in 1530 looking for gold and the expansion of their empire. The Incas were terrified into submission by the Spanish with their horses and guns, and their empire dissolved in a few short years. Their communications system was destroyed and families returned to subsistence farming. At this time, European livestock such as pigs, goats and poultry were brought to Peru, as well as crops such as rice that were previously unknown in South America. The Spanish found gold, silver, precious gems and a fertile country with its own well-developed agriculture, which they promptly exploited for their own gain for nearly 300 years, until the people of Peru reclaimed their independence in 1821.

Later immigrants

Peru is now such a melting pot of nationalities that it is amazing that any of the old traditions survive. However, since the Spanish incursion, new races have been welcomed and there has been much intermingling of families and customs, leading to a new Peru with an interest in many countries of the world. First, the Spanish conquerors brought African slaves to work for them, especially as cooks. The African influence has been noticeable in some Peruvian dishes such as the special festival sweet, turron de Dona Pepa, as well as anticuchos, tamales and picarones, originally snacks sold on the streets by the slaves to raise money. Once slavery was abolished in the 19th century, the Chinese followed to take over the cooking role in Peruvian kitchens and brought their own interest in fresh vegetables and spicy tastes. Europeans followed in the 20th century, escaping from world wars and the Spanish Civil War, and again brought culinary traditions which were embraced by the Peruvians.

Peru's geography and climate

The enchanting country of Peru lies on the west coast of the South American continent. It covers a large area, from the equatorial north to the temperate south, and is made up of an incredibly diverse terrain, from its long, straight coastline, which faces south-west into the Pacific Ocean, to the snow-topped Andes mountains. Between these two extremes Peru enjoys an amazing variety of geography and climate, conditions which have led to its high biodiversity.

A diverse climate

Three very distinct geographical regions run the length of the country: the western coastal strip, with many small rivers and streams tumbling through on their way to the Pacific Ocean; the Andes mountains, forming the backbone of Peru; and to the east, the rainforest, an exuberant and fertile region where the Amazon River rises before making its way slowly and steadily to the Atlantic.

Peru just touches the Equator at its northern edge. The departments of Piura and Tumbes in the north naturally experience very high temperatures, but the Andes Mountains modify the heat over most of the country and stop the rain sweeping in from the Atlantic Ocean. The Pacific Ocean, on the western side, brings a pleasantly soft climate.

Peru has an enormous diversity of climates within one country – it actually experiences 28 of the 32 officially recognized climate types of the whole world. This means that the agricultural contribution that Peru makes to the world is enormous: hundreds of varieties of potato, corn, peanuts, chilli, strawberries and other crops are grown in this amazingly varied landscape.

Other crops such as lucuma, palmito, yacon and mashua are beloved of Peruvians but almost unknown elsewhere in the world. Indeed, even within Peru some of these local favourites are unfamiliar in neighbouring regions. In Lima, the capital city, the abundant cornucopia of produce is presented for sale in the vibrant markets.

The coastal strip

The green-blue Pacific bathes the golden sandy beaches, and rivers pour down from the mountains to join the ocean, leaving wonderfully fertile green river valleys. This is an ideal country for agricultural production. Starting in the hot north, algarrobo trees lend a welcome patch of green shade; here the sea gives a harvest of prawns (shrimp) and scallops.

Above: The combination of tropical latitude, various mountain ranges, topography variations and two ocean currents gives Peru a unique variety of climates.

Above: Ancient terracing below a ruined Inca fortress on a hillside above Pisac, Peru.

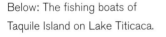
Below: The fishing boats of Taquile Island on Lake Titicaca.

Above: A farmer ploughs his field of corn in the warm south, near Nazca.

Further north, where the climate is milder, there are plantations of coconut palms, bananas, pineapples, limes and mangoes. Goats, cows, pigs and sheep graze in the verdant river valleys.

The central part of the coastal strip is very humid. Farmers here grow sugar cane, rice, corn, cotton, wheat, barley, potatoes and asparagus, as well as many other vegetables and fruits. Further south, the climate becomes drier. Olives and vines flourish, and the towns cluster around the sea, where fishing has traditionally been the population's lifeline.

The high Andes
In the extreme heights and gentle foothills of the vast Andes, the Peruvian people have learned to live with the wide variations in temperature and difficult climate of a mountain range. It is very hot and dry in the daytime where the sun strikes the ground; cold in the shade of the mountains; and freezing at night. Older people and those in the more remote villages still dress as their ancestors did, the men in a woollen poncho and the women in tall hats and layered skirts, often richly embroidered around the hem.

Cocoa and coffee beans are grown on the mountain slopes, and minerals such as gold and silver can be found deep in the mines. Further south, where the mountains open out to the rainforest in the central region, different crops are grown, such as avocados, bananas and citrus fruits. In the far south of the Andes, Lake Titicaca gives a rich harvest of freshwater fish, which the local people depend on for their livelihood.

The remote rainforest
This is a totally different world from the rest of Peru, completely based on water and the land's relationship with it. Rivers form the main communication routes in the wilder areas, and everyone travels by canoe. The people do their best to maintain their traditions, living by hunting and fishing, and guarding their knowledge of plants' medicinal properties.

Peruvian cuisine

To the untrained eye, Peruvian recipes can appear simple and repetitive, especially when most of them seem to include potato and corn in some way. However, to Peruvian tastebuds, there is a world of difference between one subtly flavoured dish and another. This variation may come simply from using one particular herb, spice or vegetable rather than another, or by adding a different dressing to a finished dish. Peruvian cuisine relies on cooking basic recipes with an almost infinite number of creative variations according to what is available in the market.

A culinary treasure-house

It is said that cooks in Peru can make three meals a day for a year without precisely repeating any one of those meals, such is the delightful variety of ingredients to be found in this geographically diverse country. The taste, appearance, smell and texture of a dish of ceviche (raw fish or shellfish marinated in citrus juice), for example, will seem totally different from place to place and from day to day, depending on which kind of fish has been caught and how it has been dressed. Only the preparation will be the same, a method handed down for hundreds of years and refined by the influence of Japanese immigrants in the 20th century. When you consider that at least six hundred kinds of fish and shellfish can be found in the Pacific

Right: A typical outdoor market in Cuzco.

Below: A fishing boat returning to harbour off the island of Lobos de Afuera.

Above: Alfresco eating outside a restaurant in Arequipa.

Above right: Corn cobs are cooked and sold in the streets.

Below: A little Peruvian girl eating freshly baked cookies from the market in Pisac.

Ocean near Peru, not to mention the river fish from the highlands and the Amazon basin, the possibilities seem endless.

Peruvians have a fine palate, as they are used to eating excellent quality ingredients. Even the taste of a boiled potato can be varied by adding butter, olive oil or chilli to it, using one of the more than three thousand varieties of potato recognized by the International Potato Institute. The same thing happens with corn, another staple food, which also has a large number of Peruvian varieties. A simple dish of corn on the cob prepared in the coastal area will taste totally different from one made in the mountains.

Mealtime routines

Bearing in mind the range of ingredients available to the Peruvian cook, it is not surprising that this cuisine is respected worldwide. One thing that all Peruvian recipes have in common is the reliance on fresh ingredients, and it is this that dictates what is eaten each day.

Some of the formal dining traditions of the Inca empire survived the Spanish conquest, particularly in the importance placed on most family meals, apart from breakfast. These days breakfast can be sketchy, and is often a simple matter of a milky drink (coffee, cocoa or plain hot or cold milk) and bread, eaten quickly before dashing off to school or to work. If they have time, some Peruvians will cook porridge for breakfast as they do in North America, but still with lots of milk, and topped with sugar or jam. At weekends families tend to gather for a later, more extensive breakfast of tamales, chicharrones, or sandwiches filled with ham, cheese or sausage, served with plenty of coffee.

People tend to sit quite formally at the table to eat their main meal of the day, although snacks are very popular in between, often eaten casually on the move in the street. Time is put aside for a proper meal, usually at lunchtime, and often in the company of family or friends. Weekday evening meals are a shorter, quieter affair to round off the day.

At every meal, there is bread on the table. Peruvians love French rolls and buy them from the bakery sometimes twice a day to ensure that they are completely fresh and of the best quality. The bread rolls and a soft drink such as lemonade, orange or passion fruit juice, barley water or the famous chicha morada will be set out for everyone to serve themselves as they arrive.

Apart from a dish of rice, which is a staple at dinner time, there will usually be a sauce based on chilli, onion or cheese to accompany the food, and sometimes a large bowl of salad. Peruvian cooks pride themselves on seasoning their dishes correctly before they are served, so salt and pepper will not normally appear on the table – the flavour should already be just right.

Soups and first courses

A bowl of soup is a favourite in Peru, and there are plenty of options, from a nutritious clear soup based on a good stock, a simple peasant soup of just three or four ingredients, to a really hearty dish with plenty of sustenance for a hard-working farmer, herdsman or fisherman. The latter soups are a meal in themselves, and are usually served as such, rather than as an appetizer.

At an elaborate family meal, or when guests are visiting, appetizers are served before the main course, and these are also dishes that people love to eat as snacks. Small morsels of raw marinated fish (ceviche), corn dumplings

cooked in banana leaves (tamales), sweet corn parcels baked inside the husks (humitas), little filled pastries (empanaditas) – these are just a few examples of the appetizers and snacks to be found in Peru.

The main course

Stews and casseroles are a favourite main course, particularly vegetable concoctions including potatoes, corn and squash, topped with cheese. These might contain added protein in the form of pork, poultry, beef, fish or shellfish, while recipes based on larger amounts of meat such as slices of beef or chicken sometimes have an egg on top. Locally grown spices such as chilli and turmeric add a kick to the simplest recipe. These substantial dishes are almost always accompanied by rice, which grows in great abundance in the damp, warm climate of the coastal area. Peruvians adore rice, they consider it softens and enhances the flavour of a main dish and helps the different ingredients to harmonize with each other.

Something sweet

When it comes to desserts and puddings, another whole area of culinary creativity opens up. Ice cream is made in many different flavours, including some that non-Peruvians might not recognize, such as lucuma. This tropical yellow-orange fruit lends its individual

Above: Most main meals will include potatoes, and in Peru there are many varieties to choose from.

Above left: Freshly baked empanadas, the delicious snack introduced by the Spanish.

Below: Piles of fresh bread for sale outside the oven of a bakery in Pisac.

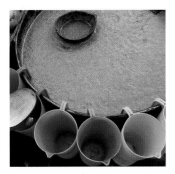

Above: Chicha ready to be measured out for sale.

Below: Purple corn powder for making chicha morada.

flavour and colour to a popular dessert that is wonderfully refreshing in the hot climate. There are also innumerable recipes for preserving fruits in syrup, a technique that arose from the thrifty tradition of previous generations. Apart from fruit-based desserts, Peruvians love to eat sponge or pastry dishes with fruit fillings, or milk-based puddings such as suspiro a la Limena ('the sigh of a woman from Lima'), which is a delicate confection of milky custard (manjar blanco) and light meringue flavoured with vanilla, or picarones, a sautéed dough made of squash and sweet potato drizzled with molasses and fig syrup.

Chicha

During the pre-Inca and Inca years in Peru, the main beverage drunk in both town and countryside was chicha, a brewed grain drink containing varying degrees of alcohol. Children tended to drink it fresh while adults preferred it properly brewed, with a stronger taste and higher alcohol level. Chicha survived the Spanish conquest and is still the preferred drink of indigenous people.

The rather sour flavour is definitely an acquired taste. In Arequipa in the far south, chicha is red, but in the rest of Peru it is a golden straw colour, varying in shade depending on the ingredients used – maize, wheat, barley, quinoa, or vegetables such as cassava or beans.

Alcoholic drinks

When the Spanish arrived in the 16th century, they brought their excellent wine with them. Grape vines were immediately established in Peru, and it was soon found that a beautiful white spirit could be distilled from the grapes. This punchy, strongly alcoholic drink is sold as 'pisco', after the town from which it was originally exported. Wine production began later and focused on red varieties, which perfectly accompany Peru's red meat dishes.

Since its introduction in the 19th century, beer has become part of Peruvian life and part of the cuisine. It is commonly served with a meal at home with the family, and to some extent has taken the place of chicha.

Non-alcoholic drinks

For those who prefer soft drinks, there is a vast range of delicious juices made of all kinds of Peruvian fruits, for instance papaya, mango, pineapple or citrus fruits. Chicha morada is a distinctive sweet, non-alcoholic version of chicha, based on the purple corn of the valleys of the Andes mountains; it can be bought as a dried powder as well as fresh.

The Peruvian table

In traditional families, the dining table is laid with a good quality cloth, napkins, silverware and plates in accordance with the number of dishes to be served. Obviously for the many festive dinners a more elaborate setting is appropriate, with many courses needing a corresponding number of knives and forks, glasses and serving dishes. In urban areas in particular, setting the table in the correct way is a sign of breeding and education, rather than wealth. There are subtle differences, for instance, between a tablecloth that is deemed suitable for tea and one that is used for dinner. A buffet is set out less formally, in North American style, but still with enough dishes, plates and silverware of the best quality.

Festivals and celebrations

In present-day Peru, many religious festivals punctuate the year. This is a land where over 80 per cent of the people are now Catholics, and the major saints' days and the calendar of the religious year dictate what food is to be eaten and how each festival is to be celebrated. However, underlying the Christian rituals is an older rhythm linked to the Inca tribes, whose celebrations were based on thanking and propitiating the gods of harvest, weather and the sun.

New Year

Parties to celebrate the new year start during the evening of 31 December, and the music and dancing usually lasts until the next morning. On 1 January, many people eat a traditional breakfast of chicharrones (fried pork strips) and tamales (steamed corn wraps with meat or cheese filling), or head for the beaches where there are stalls offering ceviche (a spicy fish dish) as a hangover cure.

Carnival

February is carnival month in Peru. The city of Ayacucho is renowned for its elaborate celebrations, marking the period of freedom and excess before the restraints of Lent. The most famous carnival foods are chicharrones, tamales, and pachamanca (a joint of meat – sometimes a whole carcass). These are all baked under hot stones in huge temporary ovens constructed in the street.

Incas and Catholics

The Inca people of Peru felt the importance of giving thanks for a good harvest, as their prosperity was linked to the success of their farming. Nothing was taken from the land without asking the permission of the gods and acknowledging their favours. Even minor details such as maintaining irrigation ditches were turned into rituals.

After the Spanish conquest, Inca rituals gradually disappeared as the people converted to Christianity. However, some ancient festivals were hidden within or incorporated into the new religious ones. Today there is space for more secular celebrations amid the Christian festivals.

Easter

Processions and church services are focused on Lenten penance and fasting until the joyous release of Easter Sunday. The special Easter dishes eaten in Peru are usually based on fish and shellfish. A real favourite at this time is Spanish-influenced bacalao (salted cod) mixed with chickpeas and (bell) peppers.

Below left: Potatoes are cooked at a street carnival.

Below middle: Women in a Lord of the Miracles procession.

Below: A typically flamboyant costume in an Easter parade.

Above: The procession to celebrate Inti Raymi or the Festival of the Sun in Cuzco.

Below: Characters in a street parade at Corpus Christi.

Above: Special types of bread are baked for All Souls' Day and entered in competitions.

Above: Turron de Dona Pepa, made especially for eating at the festival of the Lord of the Miracles.

Cuzco jubilee

There are two major ceremonies in Cuzco in June, Corpus Christi – a Catholic religious ritual – and at the same time, Inti Raymi, an Inca festival when people of Cuzco honour the sun, the earth and its produce, particularly corn. The main dish is chiri uchu (chicken, guinea pig, corn omelette, cheese and black pudding, served cold on a large platter), accompanied by chicha de jora (a corn beverage that dates back to the Inca period).

Spring festivals

The beginning of the rainy season in August is celebrated just as the Incas used to do, with the cleaning of irrigation channels and wells. Lamb stew is a favourite dish at this time. In Apurimac, the Virgin of Cocharcas is celebrated on 8th September with a procession and feasting on springtime dishes such as huatia (potatoes cooked under hot stones), japchi (fresh cheese with spring onions, broad beans, peas and lettuce) and picantes (stew with garlic, onions and chilli).

The Lord of the Miracles

In October, there is a major festival in Lima: the three processions of the Lord of the Miracles. This brings together more pious worshippers, dressed in purple, than the streets can hold. Special dishes include a delicious golden sweet called turron de Dona Pepa, made of sugar and syrup of fig leaves. There are other delights too, such as chicha morada, a beverage made with purple corn and fruits, and mazamorra morada, a purple corn pudding made of the same mixture, thickened with potato starch.

All Souls' Day

In November everyone in Peru celebrates All Souls' Day to commemorate the dead. People spend the whole night in vigil, and take flowers to the tombs of family and friends. The cemeteries are full of visitors and in some towns the visitors bring music, food and presents for the dead, as the Incas believed that they still need sustenance in the afterlife.

Christmas

The main meal of Christmas is eaten after midnight mass (now sometimes celebrated earlier, at 10 p.m.) on Christmas Eve. The menu is really lavish: tamales, stuffed roast turkey, salads and apple sauce, a North American introduction. During Christmas Day itself, Peruvian hot chocolate – the best in the world – and Italian panettone is served.

Classic ingredients

In Peru it is the custom, but also a matter of personal pride, for the cook of the family to shop nearly every day at the market. Meals are concocted almost entirely from fresh, local, seasonal ingredients of the best possible quality. Only a few ingredients, such as milk, can be bought canned or pre-packed; otherwise it is a matter of seeing what is in store or at the market each day and using these ingredients as the basis for an excellent meal.

Peruvian markets

In every town there are various markets, from the deluxe ones selling nothing but the most expensive ingredients to the popular markets offering bargains that are often still of good quality. Nowadays there are also some supermarkets where the shelves are full of food and household necessities, but the traditional markets still attract more people because they sell at a better price, and because in smaller towns and rural communities they are often an important social, as well as shopping, experience.

Meat and poultry

These days most types of meat are available in all regions of Peru. Markets carry a good range, including the popular guinea pig, once an Andean delicacy but now enjoyed all over the country fried (chactado or frito), grilled or broiled (asado), or roasted (al horno).

Beef is another popular meat, and all parts of the animal are used; many Peruvian dishes are based on beef heart, liver, tripe and kidneys. These are sold at a low price and are

extremely nutritious. When it comes to pork, the same applies: every part of the pig is cooked, in traditional thrifty fashion. All the basic cuts such as pork joints and chops are available for main meals; the lesser cuts are usually made into sausages, bacon or black pudding (blood sausage) with herbs.

Above: Going to the market is a leisurely experience at the weekend, often involving the whole family, like here in Pisac.

Below, left to right: Duck legs, rabbit, tripe and chicken.

Above: Some of Peru's much-loved seafood, from top to bottom; clams, halibut, crayfish and prawns.

Above right: Fresh cheese has a mild flavour and soft texture.

Lamb tends to be eaten mainly in the centre and south of Peru, in the high mountainous regions where sheep thrive in the rocky terrain, while goat is still sometimes eaten in the north. Sometimes in the markets prepared dishes of lamb or goat are available, or fresh meat already marinated for cooking.

Chicken is a staple of Peruvian cuisine. Peruvians eat it in many guises: old tough birds were traditionally stewed to tenderize them, and then used in a range of imaginative salads. There is at least one stall in even the smallest market dedicated to this nutritious meat. Llama, once eaten by Incas, is still enjoyed, especially dried as 'charqui', which is used to flavour many dishes. Another traditional meat, rabbit, is less common these days, but still enjoyed when available.

Fish and shellfish

Specialist fish counters offer fantastic fresh produce in every market, with the best specimens sold whole. Good fishmongers will clean and cut fish to order, as well as keeping a good supply of prepared fillets ready to be weighed and sold.

There are so many varieties of fish available in Peru, with its long coastline facing the warm Pacific Ocean and its wide inland rivers, that it would be impossible to list them all; it has been estimated that there are 2,000 species in Peruvian waters. Two of the most popular are sea bass and lemon sole, both of which have a delicate flavour that is perfect served with a wide range of seasonings and sauces. Many of the fish eaten in Peru are not well known in other countries, but the recipes for them work well with most white fish.

Shellfish and molluscs are also found in abundance, from prawns (shrimp), crayfish, squid and octopus to scallops, mussels and whelks, all of which are transformed into delicious dishes with the addition of wonderful sauces. Many of these spiced dishes just need a bland accompaniment such as rice or potatoes to complement their piquant flavour.

Dairy produce

Peruvians love creamy food, and milk is often added to soups, stews, puddings and drinks. Canned condensed milk is often used instead of fresh. A good range of cheeses are made in the different regions of Peru according to local customs and the kind of milk available – from cows, sheep or goats.

Fresh cheese is a young, soft white cheese sprinkled with salt that is typical of traditional Peruvian cuisine and comes from the mountains, in the central Mantaro region. It is used to prepare creamy sauces such as 'ocopa' or 'huancaina', or simply sliced and served with a hot, freshly cooked corn cob. The cheese from the northern mountains, especially from the town of Cajamarca, has a distinctive taste and texture. It is creamy and buttery, and melts easily when heated. Peruvians love to eat fresh butter with bread, but margarine is more often used in baking.

Pulses, grains and nuts

Dried beans, lentils and cereals are a basic, cheap, nourishing food found in many homes. Butter (lima) beans, red and green lentils, chickpeas, dried green peas, quinoa, and the

very Peruvian 'canario' (canary beans) with their yellowish colour and unique taste, are all widely available. Grains such as corn, rice and wheat also form a major part of the diet, whether they are used whole in stews and soups for bulk or ground into flour to make the bread that appears on every table. Corn on the cob is grown everywhere in Peru and is also eaten in many different ways, whether as a main ingredient or accompanying other dishes, or even on its own with butter, as well as forming the basis of chicha, the Peruvians' favourite national drink.

Nuts such as pecans and peanuts are treated more as snacks. Peruvians are also very fond of crisps (chips), not always made with potatoes – they are also popular made with sweet potato, plantain or cassava.

Below: Pumpkin and butternut squash.

Vegetables

Every market has several vegetable stalls, and with their vivid colour contrasts they are a real delight to the eye. Potatoes are one of the basic ingredients of Peruvian cooking – without either potatoes or rice to mop up the sauce, no main meal is considered to be complete. There are many varieties of potato, each with its own unique characteristics. Yellow potatoes are floury and tend to crumble; these are best suited to spicy marinades with chilli. White potatoes are firmer and cook well in stews and soups without falling apart. 'Huayro' potatoes are softer, with a hint of sweetness, and are ideally served as a side dish so that their flavour can be properly appreciated. And there are so many more.

After the staple potato, tomatoes are the most popular vegetable in Peruvian cuisine. They are served hot or cold, cooked or raw, made into sauces and marinades or simply dressed with oil. All sizes are for sale, from tasty plum tomatoes right up to the giant beefsteak varieties. Onions and garlic often feature in dressings or marinades, with or without tomatoes. They are the basis of many stews and soups, helping to bring out the flavour of the other ingredients.

There are many kinds of green leaves sold as salad vegetables or for cooking, for example varieties of lettuce and spinach. These leaves generally complement the sturdier vegetables such as cucumber, squash and red sweet peppers. Peruvian recipes use all kinds of squash, including small and large

Above, from left to right: Annatto seeds, butter (lima) beans, quinoa and split green peas.

Below, from top to bottom: Cassava, cabbage and dried yellow chillies.

Above, from top to bottom: Papaya, camu camu berries and mango.

Below: Turmeric, the bright yellow spice that adds a lovely earthy flavour as well as a rich colour to soups and stews.

courgettes (zucchini), medium-sized butternut squash, and pumpkins, which can grow to an enormous size. Sweet potatoes are a versatile vegetable that blends with both sweet and savoury flavours, giving a lift to both.

Cassava and plantain are favourites of the people of the rainforest, and grow well there in the steamy heat.

Fruit

Like the vegetable stalls, fruit stalls are full of different colours and aromas. The important principle when buying fruit is very simple: any fruit that does not have a strong smell is not ripe; any fruit that does not have a strong colour is not sweet. Any Peruvian coming to a fruit counter will want to sniff the peaches, papayas, melons, pineapples, apples, mangoes and plums. The few fruits that do not give off a sweet smell because of their thick skins, such as granadillas, passion fruit and watermelons, can be selected by feel – they should feel heavy – and sometimes by colour.

As well as the fruits available in most parts of the world, Peru has species that are unknown elsewhere, such as camu camu, lucuma, cocona and aguaje.

Above: A fruit stall in Cuzco's covered market.

Herbs and spices

Although many herbs and spices are used in Peruvian recipes, the most important is undoubtedly the chilli pepper. The first chillis were native to the Andes, and eaten by the men and women who lived there thousands of years ago. In Peru, the chilli is almost a sacred ingredient, symbolizing wealth and strength. Even now, men will encourage each other to add chilli to their food as a test of their virility.

Spice counters in the markets sell some ingredients ready prepared, such as peeled garlic, chilli sauces and dressings both fresh and dried, cinnamon, salt, turmeric, cumin, saffron and ginger. Many of these are known to have been consumed by the Incas; others were imported by African or Chinese cooks.

The herbs used in Peru are a good mixture of indigenous varieties, especially all kinds of mint, and those brought by the Spanish in the 16th century. Coriander (cilantro), and the various flavours of parsley and mint, basil, saffron and rosemary enhance many dishes, and are used in dressings and marinades alongside the stronger onion and garlic.

Appetizers, snacks and drinks

A formal meal in Peru often includes an appetizer, and there is a wide repertoire of much-loved and delicious little dishes and snacks in Peruvian cuisine.

Tasty little dishes to tempt the appetite

Peruvian first-course dishes are generally not filling or heavy, but are proudly presented with taste and elegance so that they tempt the eye as well as the taste buds. Many dishes feature potatoes dressed in delicious sauces with fresh cheese or chilli, while others are prepared with all kinds of fish, chicken or vegetables. Most are served cold and make a refreshing beginning to a meal in the hot climate.

Large receptions and festive celebrations are standing affairs these days with drinks, accompanied by trays of assorted canapés served by waiters, followed by a buffet spread. Years ago, in the big houses of the colonial era, all the guests would be seated for a formal dinner consisting of 20 different dishes or more, depending on the wealth and status of the host, but this tradition has been superseded by a more practical and relaxed party style. Snacks to be eaten at buffet parties are very varied, from small, delicate sandwiches to stuffed pastries (empanaditas) from corn on the cob to fried cassava with sauce – the list is endless and Peruvian cooks are happy to show how inventive they are.

As guests arrive for a formal dinner or a buffet party they will often be offered cocktails, perhaps accompanied by small and tasty appetizers, but nothing that will spoil the appetite for the feast to come. The cocktails at parties look elegant, taste delicious, and often include pisco. The Spanish introduced grapes to Peru, but wine-making was forbidden, so the local people learned to distil one clear, alcoholic spirit from grapes, which they called pisco, and another from sugar cane: rum. Both these spirits are ideally suited to cocktails, adding a rich taste and sweetness. Peruvians love them mixed with milk and eggs, and topped with the many luscious native fruits.

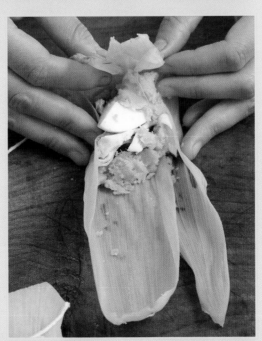

Peruvian beef pies
Empanaditas

Empanadas have been part of Peru's culinary history since the first days of Spanish rule. The little pies filled with beef, chicken or cheese make very popular mid-morning snacks and are sold in bakeries and from street stalls all over the country. Bakers have them ready at 10am, and they are sold wrapped in a paper napkin to eat straight away, with a squeeze of lime and accompanied by a glass of chicha morada or an Inca kola. These miniature versions make wonderful party appetizers.

1 To make the filling, heat the oil in a large frying pan and fry the minced beef for 5–10 minutes, stirring, until browned. Stir in the onion and fry until it is starting to caramelize, then add the raisins and olives.

2 Add the water to the pan and season to taste with salt. Cover and simmer for 10 minutes, then remove from the heat and leave to cool while you make the pastry.

3 Sift the flour into a large mixing bowl and add the salt. Rub in the margarine with your fingers. Add the water and knead until the dough is smooth and not sticky. Cover the bowl with a clean dish towel or clear film (plastic wrap) and leave it to rest for 15 minutes. Preheat the oven to 200°C/400°F/Gas 6.

4 Roll out the dough thinly on a floured surface and cut out 6cm/2½in circles using a plain cookie cutter. Spoon a little of the cooled filling (avoiding any liquid) on to each circle and add a piece of hard-boiled egg.

5 Fold the dough circle in half over the stuffing, wet the rim with a little water and pinch the edges together with your fingers. Place on an oiled baking tray, well spaced so the pies have space to spread. Bake for 15 minutes or until they are golden.

6 Leave the pastries on the tray to cool. Dust with sifted icing sugar before serving. Eat with the fingers.

Makes 20 small pies

For the filling:

75ml/5 tbsp vegetable oil

450g/1lb/2 cups minced (ground) beef

1 large red onion, finely chopped

150g/5oz/1 cup raisins, chopped

150g/5oz/1 cup kalamata olives, pitted and chopped

250ml/8fl oz/1 cup water

3 hard-boiled eggs, diced

salt

For the pastry:

450g/1lb self-raising (self-rising) flour

1.5ml/¼ tsp salt

150g/5oz margarine

60ml/4 tbsp water

150g/5oz/1¼ cups icing (confectioners') sugar

Energy 223kcal/930kJ; Protein 8g; Carbohydrate 15.3g, of which sugars 0.9g; Fat 14.9g, of which saturates 4.8g; Cholesterol 27mg; Calcium 26mg; Fibre 0.8g; Sodium 61mg.

Fried pork with onion salsa
Chicharrones

This is one of the most famous of all Peruvian dishes. Food stores and stalls cook it in huge pans called pailas, which will hold a whole quarter of pork cut into pieces. For breakfast it's eaten in a sandwich with fried sliced sweet potato and onion salsa; at lunchtime it is often served on a plate accompanied by boiled cassava.

1 Put the pork in a large pan and add the salt and just enough water to cover the meat. Bring to the boil and leave to simmer, uncovered, until all the water has evaporated.

2 Meanwhile, make the onion salsa. Put the sliced onion in a dish and sprinkle with 15ml/ 1 tbsp salt. Place a plate on top and weight it down with something heavy. Leave for 10–15 minutes until the onion has released its juices,

then rinse off the salt and drain thoroughly, squeezing out the liquid. Repeat, then add the lime juice, oil, sliced chilli and a pinch of salt.

3 Once the water has boiled off the pork, continue to cook the meat gently so that it fries in its own fat. Turn the pieces until they are golden on all sides. Serve the chicharrones accompanied by the onion salsa and fried sliced sweet potatoes.

Serves 8

1kg/2¼lb pork belly, cut into 2.5cm/1in squares

5ml/1 tsp salt

1 litre/1¾ pints/4 cups water

fried sliced sweet potatoes, to serve

For the onion salsa:

1 red onion, sliced

juice of 1 lime

30ml/2 tbsp vegetable oil

1 chilli, seeded and thinly sliced

salt

Energy 510kcal/2107kJ; Protein 19.4g; Carbohydrate 2g, of which sugars 1.4g; Fat 47.2g, of which saturates 16.7g; Cholesterol 90mg; Calcium 16mg; Fibre 0.4g; Sodium 92mg.

Ox heart skewers
Anticuchos

Makes 14 skewers

1 large ox heart

4 garlic cloves, peeled and chopped

45ml/3 tbsp red chilli sauce

250ml/8fl oz/1 cup red wine vinegar

5ml/1 tsp ground cumin

2.5ml/½ tsp ground annatto seeds (or 5ml/1 tsp paprika combined with 2.5ml/½ tsp turmeric)

2.5ml/½ tsp ground black pepper

5ml/1 tsp salt

60ml/4 tbsp vegetable oil

The simplicity of this dish is typical of the Peruvian style of cooking, allowing the flavour of the main ingredient to dominate, while the chilli enhances it. Ox heart can be tough, so you need to marinate it for at least 12 hours before cooking. Serve with chilli salsa and corn and accompany with very cold beer or chicha morada.

1 About 12 hours in advance, clean the heart, using a sharp knife to remove all fat and veins, and cut into 2cm/¾in pieces. Put the meat in a large bowl and add the garlic, chilli sauce, vinegar and spices. Stir well and leave in a cool place to marinate. Prepare the barbecue.

2 Thread four to six pieces of meat on each skewer. Blend 250ml/8fl oz of the marinade with the vegetable oil.

3 When the barbecue is ready, place the skewers on an oiled rack and cook for about 15 minutes until browned, turning from time to time and brushing with the marinade mixture.

Variation Serve with a chilli salsa; mix 60ml/ 4 tbsp chilli sauce with the same amount of the marinade and 4 chopped spring onions (scallions) in a pan. Bring to the boil, simmer for 5 minutes, then pour into a bowl to serve.

Energy 150kcal/630kJ; Protein 20.5g; Carbohydrate 1.1g, of which sugars 0.7g; Fat 7.1g, of which saturates 2.2g; Cholesterol 150mg; Calcium 8mg; Fibre 0g; Sodium 138mg.

Callao-style mussels
Choros a la Chalaca

Serves 4

20 New Zealand greenshell mussels, defrosted overnight in the refrigerator if using frozen

1 corn cob

1 medium red onion, very finely chopped

2 chillies, seeded and finely chopped

15ml/1 tbsp finely chopped parsley

juice of 1 lime or ½ lemon

45ml/3 tbsp vegetable oil

salt and ground black pepper

lime wedges, to serve

Mussels from the Pacific coast are unique. If you are able to buy them fresh they produce a delicious stock when cooked, but for most of us they can only be bought frozen. Some Peruvians prefer to cut away the dark stomach area before serving.

1 Scrub the mussels and remove the beards. Discard any that are open and fail to close when tapped. Put in a large pan with a little water and bring to the boil over a high heat. Cook for 5–10 minutes until all the shells have opened. Drain the mussels (the stock can be frozen for another seafood dish) and remove one side of each shell, leaving the mussel in the other half. Discard any mussels that fail to open. Omit this step if using frozen mussels.

2 Boil the corn on the cob in unsalted water for about 10 minutes, until tender, then drain and slice off the kernels.

3 Put the corn in a bowl with the onion, chillies and parsley and add the lime or lemon juice, salt and pepper. Leave the mixture for 15 minutes for the flavours to infuse.

4 Arrange the mussels in their shells on a serving plate and spoon a little of the mixture on top of each mussel. Serve as canapés with lime wedges on the side.

Variation Alternatively remove the mussels from their shells, cut them into bitesize pieces, stir them into the corn and onion mixture, and serve with a green salad.

Energy 128kcal/530kJ; Protein 7.7g; Carbohydrate 3.3g, of which sugars 1.5g; Fat 9.4g, of which saturates 1.4g; Cholesterol 21mg; Calcium 30mg; Fibre 0.8g; Sodium 574mg.

Marinated fish
Cebiche

This dish is mentioned in Peruvian literature from the 19th century, and its roots are much older. The raw fish is 'cooked' by the action of citrus juice, originally from sour oranges, which once grew abundantly on the coast. Cebiche, or ceviche, is now eaten all along the Pacific coast, and every country has its own version.

1 Cut the fish into bitesize pieces about 2cm/¾in across, and place in a bowl with the onion, chilli and celery. Season well with salt and pepper.

2 Pour the lime juice over the mixture and stir gently to distribute it evenly. Cover and leave to marinate for 15 minutes, then stir again and leave for another 15 minutes. The fish is ready when it has become opaque.

3 Meanwhile, boil the sweet potatoes in unsalted water for 25 minutes and boil the cassava in salted water for 20 minutes, until tender. Cut the corn on the cob into four pieces and boil in unsalted water for 10–15 minutes.

4 Arrange the lettuce leaves around the edge of a serving dish and pile the fish mixture in the middle. Serve immediately, accompanied by sweet potatoes, corn on the cob and cassava.

Cook's tip To serve cebiche as a snack to accompany drinks, cut the fish into smaller pieces and arrange spoonfuls of the mixture in small scallop shells. You may prefer to marinate the fish for more or less time: experiment with the timing to see how you like it best.

Serves 4

500g/1¼lb firm white fish fillets such as cod, halibut or coley, skinless and boneless

½ medium red onion, sliced lengthways

1 chilli, seeded and sliced

2 celery sticks, thinly sliced

juice of 8 limes, about 150ml/10 tbsp

4–8 lettuce leaves, to garnish

15ml/1 tbsp finely chopped parsley

salt and ground black pepper

To accompany:

2 medium sweet potatoes, peeled and cut into chunks

500g/1¼lb cassava, peeled and cut into chunks

1 corn on the cob

Energy 145kcal/612kJ; Protein 18.7g; Carbohydrate 9.3g, of which sugars 8.1g; Fat 4g, of which saturates 0.7g; Cholesterol 85mg; Calcium 67mg; Fibre 1.7g; Sodium 126mg.

Soused fish with onions
Escabeche de pescado

Inca methods of preparing food for storage included drying potatoes in the cold and meat in the sun, but the Spanish brought wine vinegar and sugar, which offered new ways of preserving, as well as flavouring food. They also introduced the onion. This delicious dish is at least five centuries old, and uses the preserving technique of boiling onions with vinegar, but here it is eaten as soon as it has cooled. Escabeche is popular in Panama, Mexico and Spain, as well as Peru.

Serves 4

2 medium onions, thickly sliced lengthways

500ml/17fl oz/generous 2 cups water

175ml/6fl oz/¾ cup red wine vinegar

500g/1¼lb firm-textured fish fillets, such as sea bass, bream, cod or haddock

115g/4oz plain (all-purpose) flour

200ml/7fl oz/scant 1 cup vegetable oil

4 garlic cloves, finely chopped

2 red chillies, seeded and sliced lengthways

30ml/2 tbsp red chilli sauce

2.5ml/½ tsp ground cumin

salt and ground black pepper

To accompany:

2 medium sweet potatoes

lettuce leaves

kalamata-type olives

115g/4oz feta cheese, crumbled

2 hard-boiled eggs, sliced

1 Put the onions in a pan with the water, 50ml/2fl oz/¼ cup of the vinegar and a good pinch of salt. Bring to the boil and simmer for 2 minutes, then remove from the heat, drain and set aside.

2 Cut the fish into four portions. Season the flour with pepper and salt and toss the fish in it.

3 Heat 150ml/¼ pint/⅔ cup of the oil in a frying pan over medium heat and fry the fish for about 6 minutes on each side, until cooked through, then lift the pieces out and arrange them in a shallow dish.

4 Add the remaining oil to the frying pan over medium-high heat and fry the garlic until golden. Add the boiled onions, the sliced chillies, chilli sauce and cumin, stir and add the rest of the vinegar.

5 Check the seasoning, adding more salt if necessary. Remove from the heat and pour the contents of the pan over the fish. Leave to cool.

6 Put the sweet potatoes in a pan with water to cover and boil them for 25 minutes, until they are tender. Drain, peel and slice.

7 To serve, place a lettuce leaf on each plate and spoon a portion of fish with some of the sauce on top. Add slices of sweet potato and garnish with olives, feta and hard-boiled egg.

Energy 414kcal/1720kJ; Protein 41.9g; Carbohydrate 1.3g, of which sugars 1g; Fat 26.7g, of which saturates 3.2g; Cholesterol 104mg; Calcium 30mg; Fibre 0.2g; Sodium 137mg.

Scallops with butter and Parmesan cheese
Conchitas a la Parmesana

The temperate waters in the south of Peru provide abundant scallops, which are small and tasty. Italian immigrants arrived in Peru in the 19th century, and again after World War I, and with them came Parmesan cheese.

1 Open the scallops and remove the flat half shell. Clean each one by removing the brown ring and the brown part near the white flesh. Rinse the flesh, leaving it in the shell. Preheat the oven to 180°C/350°F/Gas 4.

2 Place all the prepared scallops in a baking tray and pour a drop of lime juice into each one. Add a tiny piece of butter and sprinkle with a small spoonful of cheese.

3 Bake the scallops for 10 minutes until the cheese is bubbling and browned. Divide among four plates with strips of lime rind and wedges for a first course, or serve as canapés.

Serves 4

24 small scallops in their shells

juice of ½ lime

115g/4oz/8 tbsp butter

175g/6oz/2 cups grated Parmesan cheese

strips of lime rind and lime wedges, to garnish

Energy 557kcal/2320kJ; Protein 46.4g; Carbohydrate 4.3g, of which sugars 0g; Fat 39.6g, of which saturates 25g; Cholesterol 169mg; Calcium 566mg; Fibre 0g; Sodium 918mg.

Broad bean and fresh cheese salad
Solterito de habas

Serves 4

250g/9oz small white potatoes

250g/9oz/2 cups shelled broad (fava) beans

kernels of 1 fresh corn on the cob or 1 medium can corn in unsalted water

150g/5oz feta cheese, cut into 1cm/½in dice

15ml/1 tbsp white wine vinegar

45ml/3 tbsp olive oil

1 fresh red or green chilli, seeded and finely chopped

salt and ground black pepper

lettuce leaves, to garnish

Broad beans are very dear to the Peruvian people. They are used in soups, stews and many other dishes, and, when young and freshly picked, are eaten raw as a snack. This is a substantial salad that makes a satisfying first course. It can be made with fresh or frozen beans, but fresh young beans have the best texture.

1 Boil the potatoes in lightly salted water for 20 minutes, until tender. Drain and allow to cool for 10 minutes, then gently slide the skin off with your fingers and cut into 1cm/½in dice.

2 Boil the broad beans in lightly salted water for 15 minutes. Drain and allow to cool, then pop them out of their skins. If the beans are young and small you need not do this.

3 If using fresh corn on the cob, boil for 10 minutes, then drain and slice off the kernels with a sharp knife. Leave to cool. If using canned corn, drain it.

4 Mix the potatoes, beans and corn kernels with the cheese in a salad bowl and dress with the vinegar, oil, salt and pepper. Sprinkle the chilli on top and serve garnished with lettuce.

Cook's tip When using potatoes for salads, boil them whole in their skins to retain all their texture, flavour and nutrients. Remove the skin when cool enough to handle.

Energy 293kcal/1225kJ; Protein 12.6g; Carbohydrate 24.6g, of which sugars 4.6g; Fat 16.7g, of which saturates 6.5g; Cholesterol 26mg; Calcium 175mg; Fibre 5g; Sodium 620mg.

Spiced potato with tuna
Causa rellena con atun

Serves 4

500g/1¼lb King Edward
  potatoes

juice of 1 lime

30ml/2 tbsp chilli sauce

30ml/2 tbsp vegetable oil

5ml/1 tsp salt

lettuce leaves

4 kalamata olives

2 hard-boiled eggs, sliced

For the filling:

200g/7oz can tuna fish
  in brine

150ml/¼ pint/⅔ cup
  mayonnaise

red chilli, cut into fine strips,
  to garnish (optional)

In Peru the potato has cult status. It is eaten cold, hot, dried, in stews, on its own or with sauces or chilli. It figures in appetizers, main courses and even in some dessert recipes, and yellow potato is the first solid food for babies. This recipe is a favourite.

1 Boil the whole potatoes in lightly salted water for 20 minutes, until tender, then drain. When cool enough to handle, peel and mash to a smooth purée. Place the mashed potato in a bowl, cover and leave to get cold.

2 Meanwhile, to make the filling, drain the tuna fish thoroughly, place it in a bowl and mix with the mayonnaise. Cover and set aside.

3 When the potato is cold add the lime juice, chilli sauce, oil and salt, and beat the mixture until it is even in colour and flavour. Taste it and correct the seasoning, then leave it to rest for 5 minutes to absorb the flavours.

4 To assemble the dish, line a serving plate with lettuce leaves, then spread half the potato mixture carefully over the lettuce.

5 Spoon filling on top of the potato, and spread it evenly, then spread the remaining potato over the top, neatening the edges with a spatula or knife. Garnish with the olives, slices of egg, and fine strips of red chilli, if you wish.

Variation For a vegetarian filling, mix together a finely chopped red onion, the cooked kernels of one corn on the cob and a finely chopped, seeded chilli. Stir in the juice of a lime, 15ml/ 1 tbsp vegetable oil and 2.5ml/½ tsp salt.

Energy 490kcal/2038kJ; Protein 17.6g; Carbohydrate 22.6g, of which sugars 3.8g; Fat 37.3g, of which saturates 5.7g; Cholesterol 149mg; Calcium 31mg; Fibre 1.3g; Sodium 462mg.

Potatoes in cheese and chilli sauce
Papas a la Huancaina

The Mantaro Valley supports large herds of cattle, whose milk produces a very special queso fresco, 'fresh cheese' with a mild flavour. Peruvians enjoy it with a freshly boiled corn on the cob. Mild feta cheese can be used as a substitute.

1 Boil the potatoes in lightly salted water for 15–20 minutes, until just tender.

2 Meanwhile, put all the ingredients for the sauce into a blender or food processor and blend until smooth. Check the flavour, adding salt or chilli to taste.

3 When the potatoes are cooked, drain them and allow to cool a little, then peel while they are still warm and slice thickly.

4 Boil the corn on the cob in unsalted water for about 10 minutes, drain and cut into chunks.

5 To assemble the dish, lay one or two lettuce leaves on each plate and arrange potato slices on top, and cover with sauce. Add the olives, eggs and corn to the plate. Garnish with red chilli strips, if you wish.

Variation Serve the sauce as a dip, with baby potatoes on cocktail sticks (toothpicks).

Serves 6

1kg/2¼lb floury potatoes

2 corn on the cob

a few kalamata olives

3 hard-boiled eggs, halved

lettuce leaves

red chilli, cut into fine strips, to garnish (optional)

salt

For the sauce:

500g/1¼lb queso fresco or mild feta cheese

3 red chillies, seeded

juice of 1 lime

3 crackers

45ml/3 tbsp vegetable oil

120ml/4fl oz/½ cup milk

Energy 445kcal/1860kJ; Protein 21.2g; Carbohydrate 32.2g, of which sugars 5g; Fat 26.6g, of which saturates 13.1g; Cholesterol 155mg; Calcium 357mg; Fibre 2.3g; Sodium 1666mg.

Avocado stuffed with chicken mayonnaise
Palta a la reina

One of the culinary contributions of Central and South America is the fruit of the avocado tree. Its buttery texture and delicate taste goes well with almost everything and it can be eaten with salt or sugar, with bread, seafood, vegetables or chicken, as soup, sauce, salad, sandwich filling or vegetable. There is even a liqueur made from it. Here is a luxurious recipe for a first course.

1 Put the chicken in a pan with 1 litre/1¾ pints/4 cups water, the carrot, celery, leek and a pinch of salt. Bring to the boil. reduce the heat, cover and simmer for 30 minutes.

2 Remove the chicken from the stock and let it cool, then shred the meat finely, either with your fingers or with two forks, into a bowl and mix it with the mayonnaise.

3 Halve the avocados, remove the stones (pits), and peel them. Remove a small slice from the bottom of each half to stop it rolling.

4 Place an avocado half on individual serving plates. Sprinkle generously with salt and stuff with the chicken mixture. Garnish each avocado half with olives and strips of red pepper and serve immediately.

Serves 4

1 chicken breast fillet, skinned

1 small carrot

1 celery stick

½ small leek

250ml/8fl oz/1 cup mayonnaise

2 ripe avocados

2 kalamata olives, pitted and halved or sliced

strips of red (bell) pepper, to garnish

salt

Energy 585kcal/2412kJ; Protein 10.4g; Carbohydrate 4.3g, of which sugars 3.1g; Fat 58.5g, of which saturates 9.4g; Cholesterol 63mg; Calcium 29mg; Fibre 2.8g; Sodium 355mg.

Potatoes in peanut sauce
Papas con mani

Serves 6

500g/1¼lb white potatoes

75ml/5 tbsp vegetable oil

250g/9oz red onion, finely chopped

30ml/2 tbsp green chilli sauce (see cook's tip)

250g/9oz/2 cups shelled peanuts, ground

salt

3 hard-boiled eggs, quartered, lettuce leaves, and sections of cooked corn (optional) to serve

Peanuts have been eaten in Peru for many centuries, and are depicted in jewellery and other artefacts made by pre-Inca cultures. They are often used to make sauces for traditional Inca meats such as guinea pig, rabbit or pigs' feet, but in this recipe they partner potatoes. The dish is served warm.

1 Boil the potatoes in lightly salted water for about 25 minutes, until tender. Remove from the heat, drain and peel. Keep them warm.

2 Heat the oil in a frying pan over medium heat and fry the onion for about 10 minutes until it starts to caramelize. Add the chilli sauce and the peanuts and cook for 2–3 minutes, stirring, until all the ingredients have released their flavours. Add more oil if the sauce becomes too thick. Remove from the heat.

3 Lay one or two lettuce leaves on each plate. Slice the potatoes and pile them in the centre. Pour the sauce over the potatoes and add two quarters of egg, and sections of corn if using.

Cook's tip For green chilli sauce, remove the pith and seeds from 6 green chillies. Fry in vegetable oil with ½ chopped red onion and 2 chopped garlic cloves until the onion is soft. Add salt to taste. Remove from the heat and purée in a blender or food processor.

Energy 432kcal/1799kJ; Protein 15.8g; Carbohydrate 23.1g, of which sugars 7.2g; Fat 31.4g, of which saturates 5.2g; Cholesterol 95mg; Calcium 56mg; Fibre 4.1g; Sodium 102mg.

Corn parcels
Humitas

Corn or maize has been cultivated for more than 7,000 years in America and it is still a staple food, especially in Central America and Mexico. Fresh and dried, whole and ground, it is the main ingredient for many dishes. The Peruvian variety is distinctive, with a large white grain on a big cob. It is sweet, though not as sugary as the varieties grown in North America, and it is simply delicious.

1 Remove the husks from the corn cobs (see Cook's tip) and boil the leaves in water for 10 minutes to soften, drain and cover.

2 Heat the oil for the filling in a frying pan and fry the onion and chilli until softened. Remove from the heat, add the salt and set aside.

3 Slice the kernels from the corn cobs (reserving the cobs) and blend the kernels to a paste in a blender or food processor.

4 Melt the lard in a large pan over medium heat, and fry the garlic purée. Add the two chilli sauces, the corn paste, the cornmeal or polenta, and a pinch of salt.

5 Reduce the heat and cook the mixture for 10–15 minutes or until it forms a thick dough, stirring constantly to stop it sticking to the pan. When it is very thick, remove from the heat.

6 To prepare each parcel, spread out a piece of corn husk then lay a second piece over it, with the wide ends overlapping.

7 Spoon 30ml/2 tbsp of the corn mixture into the centre where the leaves overlap. Add a piece of chicken, some fried onion and a piece of hard-boiled egg. Cover with another 30ml/2 tbsp of corn. Fold in the sides of the leaves, then the ends, to form a rectangular parcel. Secure loosely with string as the filling will expand a little during cooking. Repeat to make seven more parcels.

8 Place the reserved corn cobs in the bottom of a large pan and pour in just enough water to cover them. Lay any remaining pieces of husk over the cobs and place the parcels on top, so they will cook in the steam. Bring to the boil and cook, covered, over a low heat for 1 hour. Remove the parcels and leave to cool for a while before opening them carefully. Serve accompanied by onion salsa.

Cook's tip Before stripping the leaves, cut around each cob about 2.5cm/1in from the bottom. Do the same at the top, then remove all the leaves, discarding the outer ones but collecting the rest for wrapping the parcels.

Makes 8 parcels

6 fresh corn cobs, with husks
125g/4¼oz lard
15ml/1 tbsp garlic purée
15ml/1 tbsp chilli sauce
15ml/1 tbsp mild chilli sauce
250g/9oz/1 cup cornmeal or fine polenta
salt
onion salsa, to serve (see page 26)

For the filling:

45ml/3 tbsp vegetable oil
1 small red onion, thickly sliced lengthways
1 small chilli, seeded and thinly sliced lengthways
2.5ml/½ tsp salt
½ cooked chicken breast fillet, shredded
2 hard-boiled eggs, quartered

Energy 429kcal/1790kJ; Protein 9.9g; Carbohydrate 45.8g, of which sugars 9.3g; Fat 23.4g, of which saturates 7.5g; Cholesterol 67mg; Calcium 22mg; Fibre 2.3g; Sodium 232mg.

Country ham sandwich
Butifarra

Makes 15 rolls

3 garlic cloves

15ml/1 tbsp annatto seeds

15ml/1 tbsp ground cumin

15ml/1 tbsp fresh or dried oregano

15ml/1 tbsp salt

1kg/2¼lb rolled leg of pork

1 medium onion, thickly sliced

To assemble:

15 French rolls

onion salsa (see page 26)

fresh red chillies, shredded

salt, to taste

Of all the different hams in Peru, this is a national favourite. Bakeries and cafés sell slices of it, carved while still warm and stuffed into a warm, freshly baked French roll with some onion salsa. If annatto seeds are unavailable, make a similar flavour by mixing together 15ml/1 tsp of paprika with 2.5ml/½ tsp of turmeric.

1 Put the garlic, annatto, cumin, oregano and salt in a blender or food processor with 250ml/8fl oz/1 cup water and blend to a paste. Pour over the pork and leave to marinate for at least 2 hours, turning it at least once.

2 Fill a large pan with water, cover, and bring it to the boil. Add the sliced onion to the pan. Remove the meat from the marinade and immerse it in the boiling water.

3 Return the water to the boil, reduce the heat and simmer, covered, for 1 hour.

4 Test the meat by piercing it with a skewer: when the juices run clear it is ready. Remove it from the stock and leave to cool before slicing.

5 To make the sandwiches, split each French roll and insert a few slices of ham together with some onion salsa, shredded chilli and salt.

Energy 266kcal/1125kJ; Protein 20.9g; Carbohydrate 37.6g, of which sugars 1.5g; Fat 4.6g, of which saturates 1.4g; Cholesterol 42mg; Calcium 94mg; Fibre 1.1g; Sodium 427mg.

Triple sandwich
Triple

Another wonderful avocado recipe, this sandwich is a delicious mix of three flavours, with the addition of mayonnaise (preferably home-made) and white bread. It could not be simpler to make, but when freshly made the result tastes really luscious. It makes a satisfying snack or light lunch.

1 Peel the avocados and remove the stones (pits). Slice the flesh thinly and sprinkle with lemon juice to stop it turning brown.

2 Spread a slice of bread with a thin layer of mayonnaise and cover with a layer of avocado slices. Sprinkle with salt.

3 Thinly spread a second slice of bread with some mayonnaise and lay it over the avocado, with the mayonnaise side down.

4 Fill the second layer of the sandwich with tomato in the same way and the third with egg, spreading the bread with mayonnaise and seasoning with salt as before. Cover with the last slice of bread.

5 Repeat with the rest of the ingredients to make five more sandwiches. Cut each one in half, remove the crusts if you prefer, and serve the sandwich immediately.

Serves 6

2 ripe avocado

lemon juice, for sprinkling

24 thin slices of good quality white bread

250ml/8fl oz/1 cup mayonnaise

4 medium tomatoes, thinly sliced

4 hard-boiled eggs, roughly chopped or sliced

salt

Energy 660kcal/2756kJ; Protein 14.6g; Carbohydrate 55.6g, of which sugars 4.6g; Fat 43.8g, of which saturates 7.5g; Cholesterol 158mg; Calcium 147mg; Fibre 3.1g; Sodium 801mg.

Pisco sour
Pisco sour

Peruvian cocktails are many and varied. Some of the ingredients are unique to Peru, such as pisco and chicha de jora (sprouted maize, cooked and fermented), while indigenous fruits such as the custard apple, guanabana (soursop) and lucuma, make good bases for cocktails. The pisco sour has acquired all-time classic status.

1 Put the egg white, gomme syrup or sugar, lime juice and ice cubes in a blender and blend until the ice is crushed. Add the pisco and blend for 1 minute.

2 Take two short cocktail glasses, and add two drops of Angostura bitters to each glass. Pour the frothy pisco and ice mixture on top, and serve immediately.

Serves 6

1 egg white

60ml/4 tbsp gomme syrup
    or sugar

juice of 2 limes

10 ice cubes

250ml/8fl oz/1 cup pisco

Angostura bitters

Energy 129kcal/540kJ; Protein 0.5g; Carbohydrate 10.5g, of which sugars 10.5g; Fat 0g, of which saturates 0g; Cholesterol 0mg; Calcium 6mg; Fibre 0g; Sodium 11mg.

Strawberry cocktail and hot milk punch
Cocktail de fresas y Ponche de leche

Another pisco-based drink, strawberry cocktail is sweetened with condensed milk, which the Peruvians love to use in both sweet and savoury recipes. This is the perfect drink for a hot summer's day. Hot milk punch, however, will warm up a winter's evening, with a delicious combination of sweet milk and spiced red wine.

Strawberry cocktail
Serves 6

125g/4¼oz/1 cup fresh strawberries, hulled

120ml/4fl oz/½ cup condensed milk

250ml/8fl oz/1 cup pisco

5 ice cubes

Hot milk punch
Serves 4

250ml/8fl oz/1 cup evaporated milk

250ml/8fl oz/1 cup red wine

1 egg

30ml/2 tbsp sugar

ground cinnamon, to dust

1 If you have time, chill the fruit and milk. To make the cocktail, place all the ingredients in a blender and blend for 3 minutes.

2 Pour the cocktail straight into glasses, adding more ice cubes if you wish, and serve straight away.

1 For hot milk punch, heat the milk in a pan or microwave to just below boiling point.

2 Put the wine, egg and sugar in a blender and blend for 1 minute.

3 Add the milk to the wine mixture, and blend for a further 30 seconds.

4 Pour into warmed glasses, dust the top with cinnamon and serve immediately.

Strawberry cocktail: Energy 160kcal/669kJ; Protein 1.9g; Carbohydrate 12.4g, of which sugars 12.4g; Fat 2g, of which saturates 1.3g; Cholesterol 7mg; Calcium 61mg; Fibre 0.2g; Sodium 29mg.
Hot milk punch Energy 157kcal/660kJ; Protein 6.6g; Carbohydrate 14.5g, of which sugars 14.5g; Fat 4g, of which saturates 2g; Cholesterol 58mg; Calcium 178mg; Fibre 0g; Sodium 96mg.

Soups

Peruvians love soups, whether it is a clear and simple first course consommé or a hearty bowl of several ingredients that is a complete meal all by itself.

Healthy, sustaining and full of goodness

Soup has been a very important part of the daily diet in Peru for centuries. The country's Spanish heritage with its pucheros (stews), blended with the ancient culinary traditions of the Inca, Aymara, and other groups, all contribute to the Peruvian taste for soup. These days there is also a desire to eat naturally and healthily, which is easy to do with a bowl of home-made soup.

In the past every piece of an animal was put to use and nothing was wasted. Once all the meat had been eaten, the skins were tanned to make leather, and the bones were boiled to make soup. Today you can still go to a Peruvian market and buy beef bones for stock: a big pan, a few litres of water and some good bones will produce a strong-tasting broth, to which you can then add vegetables and rice or pasta.

Some thin soups are just treated as the first course of a main meal, but the thick, hearty ones are a meal in themselves. There are soups made with every possible ingredient: vegetables, meat, poultry and game, fish and shellfish. However, it is quite difficult to unearth many of these homely recipes, as many Peruvians avoid serving them when they have guests for lunch or dinner. They want to present the best food they can offer, and feel that a traditional soup is too humble a dish, as it is relatively inexpensive and simple to prepare. In fact there are endless different recipes for soup in Peru, owing to the country's wide range of produce – there are said to be around 2,000 different soups made in the coastal region alone.

Some of the following recipes are very regional, while others are nationally known. Although there is not enough room for 2,000 recipes, here are some of the favourites, to give you a glimpse inside the kitchens of ordinary Peruvian families.

Clear vegetable soup
Caldo de verduras

Serves 4

250g/8oz/1½ cups green beans, trimmed

3–4 medium carrots, peeled

2 medium white potatoes, peeled

1 celery stick

1 small leek, white and pale green part only

2 vegetable stock (bouillon) cubes

salt

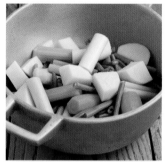

This simple soup used to be made as a kind of medicine for sick people who needed building up. Easy to digest, it helped to give them the strength to fight off illness. Although humble it is very nutritious and is excellent for the elderly, children or anyone who is under the weather and needs to avoid rich food for a few days.

1 Put the vegetables into a large pan. Add the stock cubes and 3 litres/5 pints/12½ cups water. Bring to the boil, then lower the heat to medium and cook, covered, for 25 minutes. Season with salt to taste.

2 Traditionally the soup is served separately from the vegetables, in which case strain off the broth and transfer the vegetables to a warm dish. If you serve them together you may want to chop the vegetables first.

Variations For a more filling soup; after straining the broth add 100g/3¾oz angel hair noodles and simmer until soft.

Add a beaten egg to the hot broth instead of, or as well as, the noodles.

To help settle an upset stomach, add 100g/3¾oz rice and cook it at the same time as the vegetables.

For a richer soup, blend the vegetables until smooth, return to the pan, and add some milk or cream. Reheat to serve, but do not boil.

Energy 100kcal/421kJ; Protein 3.4g; Carbohydrate 20.8g, of which sugars 8.6g; Fat 0.9g, of which saturates 0.2g; Cholesterol 0mg; Calcium 55mg; Fibre 4.6g; Sodium 32mg.

Butternut squash cream soup
Crema de zapallo

The Peruvian squash is very large, weighing as much as 20–50kg/44–110lb, and is bright yellow with a very distinctive flavour. It features in many recipes because it combines so well with potatoes and corn. This soup is made with butternut squash, which has a nutty, sweet flavour very similar to the Peruvian variety.

1 Cut the squash into small chunks, removing the seeds and hard skin. Place in a large pan with the water and bring to the boil. Cover and simmer for 15 minutes or until the squash is tender, then remove from the heat and leave to cool a little.

2 Pour the squash with its cooking liquid into a blender or food processor or use a hand blender, and blend until completely smooth.

3 Return the purée to the pan and add the milk or cream, and butter. Season to taste with salt and simmer for 1 minute.

4 Pour the soup into hot bowls and garnish with a little crumbled feta cheese or chopped hard-boiled egg. Serve with crusty bread.

Serves 4

1 butternut squash, about
   1kg/2¼lb

1 litre/1¾ pints/4 cups water

350ml/12fl oz evaporated milk
   or 250ml/8fl oz/1 cup
   single (light) cream

15ml/1 tbsp butter

50g/2oz feta cheese,
   crumbled, or 1 hard-boiled
   egg, chopped

salt

crusty French bread, to serve

Energy 185kcal/774kJ; Protein 10.6g; Carbohydrate 14.7g, of which sugars 13.5g; Fat 9.7g, of which saturates 6.2g; Cholesterol 32mg; Calcium 346mg; Fibre 2.5g; Sodium 309mg.

Butter bean soup
Sopa de pallares

Pulses are a staple food in Peru, and most people eat them at least once a week. Butter (lima) beans are grown in the south and are much appreciated for their flavour. Like most Peruvian recipes, this one concentrates on a main ingredient, with other flavourings to enhance, not disguise or overwhelm, its natural flavour.

1 Wash and drain the butter beans and put them in a large pan with 2 litres/3½ pints/ 8 cups fresh water. Bring to the boil, cover and simmer for 1 hour, until tender.

2 Meanwhile, put the potatoes in a large pan with 1 litre/1¾ pints/4 cups water and the stock cubes. Bring to the boil, cover and simmer for 15 minutes, until tender. Remove from the heat and set aside.

3 Heat the oil in a frying pan over medium heat and fry the onion with the garlic for 10 minutes, adding the paprika and oregano when they begin to caramelize. Add this mixture to the pan of potatoes and stock, then add the beans and their cooking water.

4 Bring the soup to the boil, reduce the heat and simmer for 5 minutes. Add the milk, season to taste and serve with grated cheese.

Serves 6

250g/9oz/1¼ cups butter (lima) beans, soaked overnight in plenty of water

2 large white potatoes, peeled and quartered

2 beef stock (bouillon) cubes

75ml/5 tbsp vegetable oil

1 medium red onion, finely chopped

1 garlic clove, finely chopped

2.5ml/½ tsp paprika

2.5ml/½ tsp dried oregano

250ml/8fl oz/1 cup full cream (whole) milk

45ml/3 tbsp hard, strong cheese, such as Parmesan, grated, to serve

salt

Energy 305kcal/1280kJ; Protein 14.9g; Carbohydrate 31.9g, of which sugars 4.5g; Fat 14.1g, of which saturates 3.7g; Cholesterol 13mg; Calcium 187mg; Fibre 7.4g; Sodium 241mg.

Chilca-style fish soup
Chilcano de pescado

Serves 6

2 litres/3½ pints/8 cups water

2 medium white fish, such as sea bass, about 1kg/2¼lb total weight, cleaned and gutted

2 garlic cloves, very finely chopped

1 small red onion, finely chopped

1 spring onion (scallion), finely chopped

1 red chilli, seeded and finely chopped

30ml/2 tbsp finely chopped parsley

salt and ground black pepper

1 lime, sliced, to serve

A small town to the south of Lima called Chilca has contributed the chilcano to Peruvian cooking, a fish soup enriched with lime and chilli. Sometimes it is made with the heads of the fish (an economical version once almost compulsory for students), at other times with the whole fish or with shellfish. For the soup to be a genuine chilcano it is important to make it with only one kind of fish.

1 Bring the water to the boil in a large pan with the garlic, red onion, and half the spring onion, chilli and parsley. When it bubbles, lay the fish in the pan. Season. Return to the boil, reduce the heat, cover and simmer for 10 minutes.

2 Lift out the fish and leave the soup simmering, uncovered, for a further 15–20 minutes to reduce and concentrate the flavour.

3 Meanwhile, remove the heads and tails from the fish, take off the fillets and divide into individual portions. Keep warm.

4 Strain the soup and adjust the seasoning to taste. Divide the pieces of fish among hot bowls, pour over the soup, garnish with the reserved spring onion, chilli and parsley, and serve with slices of lime.

Energy 145kcal/610kJ; Protein 31g; Carbohydrate 1.1g, of which sugars 0.8g; Fat 1.9g, of which saturates 0.7g; Cholesterol 87mg; Calcium 63mg; Fibre 0.6g; Sodium 164mg.

Seafood rice soup
Aguadito de mariscos

Aguadito is the name given to a rice soup, usually flavoured with coriander, in which the main ingredient may be meat, poultry or seafood. It comes from the north of Peru, where the climate is hot and the inhabitants are very wedded to their traditional dishes. This recipe uses the large New Zealand greenshell mussels, which you can purchase frozen in their half shells.

Serves 6

12 New Zealand greenshell mussels in half shells, fresh or frozen

12 clams

12 whole raw king prawns (jumbo shrimp)

12 small scallops

12 small squid, cleaned

45ml/3 tbsp vegetable oil

1 medium red onion, finely chopped

2 large red (bell) peppers, sliced lengthways

250g/9oz/2 cups shelled peas

large bunch of coriander (cilantro), chopped

1 whole chilli

4 litres/7 pints/16 cups water

250g/9oz/1 ¼ cups long grain rice, washed and drained

salt

1 If using fresh mussels, scrub and rinse in three changes of cold water. Scrub and rinse the clams in the same way. Discard any that are open and do not close when sharply tapped.

2 Remove the heads of the king prawns and devein them, but leave any roe intact.

3 Clean the scallops by removing the elastic part around the shell and the brown part around the scallop; it is better to keep them in their shells. Slice the squid into rings.

4 Heat the oil in a large, deep pan and fry the onion for 10 minutes until it softens and browns, add the red pepper, drained rice and peas and stir. Place the whole chilli in the pan.

5 Add the water to the pan and bring to the boil. If you are using fresh mussels, add them to the pan together with the clams. Add the coriander. Season with salt, bring back to the boil and simmer for 10–12 minutes, until the clams and mussels have opened and the rice has cooked.

6 Finally, add the squid, scallops and prawns to the pan and fold into the rice, with the mussels if using frozen. Simmer for another 3 minutes.

7 Serve the soup immediately, while piping hot, distributing the pieces of seafood evenly among the bowls. Discard any whole mussels or clams which have not fully opened.

Cook's tip Cooking the chilli whole means the flavour but not the heat is imparted to the dish. Serve with the soup, if you wish.

Energy 329kcal/1374kJ; Protein 20.7g; Carbohydrate 43.8g, of which sugars 5.3g; Fat 7.9g, of which saturates 1g; Cholesterol 135mg; Calcium 83mg; Fibre 3.5g; Sodium 193mg.

Crayfish soup
Chupe de camarones

This is one of the most special of all Peruvian dishes. The word chupe can be translated as 'chowder', and it means a hearty soup containing meat or fish, eggs, potatoes, vegetables and rice or noodles; a complete meal in one dish. In many parts of the world fishmongers sell crayfish live, in which case they are quickly immersed in boiling water, before being cleaned.

Serves 6

1kg/2¼lb fresh crayfish or Red Sea king prawns (jumbo shrimp)

75ml/5 tbsp vegetable oil

1 large tomato, diced

1 litre/1¾ pints/4 cups stock or water

6 medium floury potatoes, peeled and cut into chunks

250g/9oz butternut squash, cut into cubes

250g/9oz/1½ cups shelled and skinned broad (fava) beans

100g/3¾oz/½ cup long grain rice

2 corn cobs, cut into chunks

7.5ml/1½ tsp salt

6 eggs

350ml/12fl oz evaporated milk

1 If the crayfish are living, bring a large pan of water to the boil. Add the crayfish or prawns into the water and boil for 3–5 minutes until they change colour. Remove from the pan, reserving the stock, dry with kitchen paper, devein them, and set aside.

2 Heat the oil in a large pan over high heat and add the tomato. Cook for 2 minutes, stirring, then add 1 litre/1¾ pints/4 cups of crayfish stock, or water.

3 Add the potato, butternut squash, beans, rice, corn and salt to the pan. Bring to the boil, then lower the heat and simmer for 15 minutes, until the potatoes are almost cooked.

4 Break the eggs into the hot soup, taking care that each one stays separate from the others. Simmer for 10–15 minutes, then remove from the heat. Stir in the milk and serve, distributing the crayfish evenly and adding a poached egg to each bowl.

Energy 466kcal/1956kJ; Protein 38.2g; Carbohydrate 41.5g, of which sugars 5.9g; Fat 17.1g, of which saturates 2.9g; Cholesterol 365mg; Calcium 119mg; Fibre 4.4g; Sodium 426mg.

Hen soup from the jungle
Inchicapi de gallina

This soup comes from Amazonia, where the river floods the lowlands for half the year, then recedes leaving really fertile land for growing crops. The dish combines two major products from the region, rice and cassava. The locals would make it using a hen with a pronounced, gamey flavour, but here it has been replaced by chicken, but you could use pork, venison or other wild game.

1 Put the chicken pieces in a large pan with the water and one-third of the onion and bring to the boil, then reduce the heat, skim, and simmer for 30 minutes.

2 Grind the peanuts in a blender or food processor with the coriander leaves and 120ml/4fl oz/½ cup water, until they form a paste. Add the paste to the pan, with two-thirds of the dried oregano, the rice and cassava, and cook for a further 15 minutes. Season to taste.

3 Melt the lard in a frying pan and fry the remaining onion and the garlic until browned. Add the saffron and pour into the boiling soup. Leave to simmer for 10 minutes then serve, putting a piece of chicken and some cassava in each bowl and sprinkling with oregano.

Cook's tip Serve with an onion, chilli and tomato salsa: dice an onion and a long red chilli and mix with a diced tomato. Dress with the juice of a lime, 30ml/2 tbsp olive oil and some salt, and leave to infuse for 15 minutes.

Serves 6

1.6kg/3½lb chicken, cut into 6 pieces

3 litres/5 pints/13 cups water

1 small red onion, finely chopped

250g/9oz/2 cups shelled peanuts

small bunch fresh coriander (cilantro)

2.5ml/½ tsp dried oregano

100g/3¾oz/½ cup long grain rice

250g/9oz cassava, cut into chunks

15ml/1 tbsp lard

30ml/2 tbsp grated garlic

7.5ml/1½ tsp saffron

salt

Energy 751kcal/3123kJ; Protein 45.3g; Carbohydrate 31.8g, of which sugars 5.7g; Fat 49.5g, of which saturates 12.5g; Cholesterol 173mg; Calcium 65mg; Fibre 3.7g; Sodium 139mg.

Chicken pot with vegetables
Cazuela de gallina

Coming from the region of Tacna in the far south of Peru, this is a memorable chicken dish. In fact, every recipe from Tacna is distinctive because of the piquant seasoning used in the area's cuisine. Mooli, or daikon, has a sweet flavour that is similar to peas but the texture is more like raw potato or pear. Mooli is often eaten raw, but in a recipe where it is cooked, such as this one, you can substitute a small young turnip if you can't find mooli.

1 Joint the chicken by separating the two breast fillets from the bone, then cutting away the legs. Cut the legs to separate the drumsticks from the thighs.

2 Heat the oil in a large frying pan until it is shimmering and fry the onion, garlic and red pepper until softened. Stir in the turmeric and ginger and cook for another minute until you smell the spices. Season with salt.

3 Add the chicken pieces to the pan and cook for about 10 minutes, turning, to brown them. Transfer the onions and chicken to a large pan.

4 Add the mooli, leek, celery and carrot to the chicken in the pan and add the water. Bring to the boil, then reduce the heat and simmer for 20 minutes. Dice the potatoes, peel and dice the butternut squash, and cut the corn into 2.5cm/1in chunks.

5 Add the diced potatoes, butternut squash, peas, corn on the cob, and rice to the chicken and cook for a further 20 minutes, until the chicken and vegetables are tender.

6 Remove the pan from the heat and serve immediately, sprinkled with the chopped coriander and garnished with lime, if using.

Cook's tip A salsa made with two chillies finely diced, and chopped spring onions (scallions), with lime juice, salt and sunflower oil, can be served to accompany this dish.

Serves 6

1 chicken about 1.5kg/3¾lb
75ml/5 tbsp vegetable oil
1 medium red onion, chopped
15ml/1 tbsp grated garlic
1 red (bell) pepper, diced
5ml/1 tsp ground turmeric
5ml/1 tsp fresh ginger, grated
½ mooli (daikon), diced
1 small leek, sliced
1 celery stick, sliced
1 large carrot, diced
3 litres/5 pints/13 cups water
6 small potatoes, peeled
250g/9oz butternut squash
125g/4¼oz/1 cup shelled peas
2 corn cobs
125g/4¼oz/½ cup rice
30ml/2 tbsp fresh coriander (cilantro), finely chopped
1 lime, to garnish (optional)
salt

Energy 579kcal/2412kJ; Protein 36.8g; Carbohydrate 34.4g, of which sugars 5.9g; Fat 33g, of which saturates 7.5g; Cholesterol 165mg; Calcium 58mg; Fibre 3.7g; Sodium 504mg.

Beef hotpot
Sancochado

Sancochado is regarded as a national dish, though there are some regional variations. It developed from a Spanish dish, cocido, a substantial soup made from meats and vegetables, and is often accompanied by onion and chilli salsa.

1 Put the beef into a large pan with the water and add 15ml/1 tbsp salt, the celery heart and the cabbage. Bring to the boil, reduce the heat, skim and simmer, covered, for 45 minutes.

2 Roughly chop the potatoes, carrots, cassava and corn on the cob and add to the pan. Cook for 20 minutes. When the root vegetables are tender, lift them out with a slotted spoon, together with the celery and cabbage, and keep them warm on a serving dish.

3 Add the sweet potatoes to the soup and continue to simmer gently. When the meat and

the sweet potatoes are tender, lift them out and arrange them on the serving dish with the other vegetables.

4 Serve the broth in bowls, either adding the meat and vegetables to each bowl, or serving them separately with onion and chilli salsa.

Cook's tip While the soup is cooking keep checking that it does not reduce too much and add more water if necessary: you should finish up with about 2 litres/3½ pints/8 cups of soup. Try to keep the vegetables intact, draining them carefully when they are done.

Serves 4

1kg/2¼lb beef brisket

4 litres/7 pints/17½ cups water

1 large celery heart

1 small Savoy cabbage, halved

500g/1¼lb potatoes, peeled

500g/1¼lb carrots, peeled

500g/1¼lb cassava, peeled

2 corn on the cob

500g/1¼lb sweet potatoes, peeled

salt

Energy 709kcal/2995kJ; Protein 61.1g; Carbohydrate 81.6g, of which sugars 34.3g; Fat 17.7g, of which saturates 6.7g; Cholesterol 135mg; Calcium 217mg; Fibre 13g; Sodium 433mg.

Hearty beef soup with basil sauce
Menestrón

Serves 8

90ml/6 tbsp vegetable oil

1kg/2¼lb beef, preferably brisket, cubed

½ celery heart, sliced

½ medium leek, sliced

4 litres/7 pints/17½ cups water

½ small Savoy cabbage, sliced

150g/5oz/¾ cup shelled fresh flageolet (small cannellini) beans, or 400g/14oz can beans, drained and rinsed

150g/5oz/1 cup peeled diced carrots

200g/7oz green beans, sliced

500g/1¼lb white potatoes, diced

3 corn cobs, cut into 2.5cm/1in chunks

150g/5oz/1¼ cups penne rigati pasta

small bunch fresh basil

100g/3¾oz feta cheese

salt

This thick soup shows the influence of 19th-century Italian cuisine. The best place to eat it is in the Mantaro Valley in the central Andes Mountains, which produces the finest beef, potatoes and beans with which to prepare it.

1 Heat 75ml/5 tbsp of the oil in a large pan and brown the beef on all sides. Add the celery and leek and cook gently until soft.

2 Add the water to the pan with the cabbage and beans. Season. Bring to the boil, then reduce the heat and simmer for 30 minutes.

3 Add the diced carrots, green beans, potatoes and pieces of corn on the cob, bring back to the boil and simmer for 15 minutes.

4 Add the pasta to the pan, bring back to the boil and simmer for a further 12 minutes until the pasta is almost cooked and the meat and vegetables are tender.

5 While the pasta is cooking, strip the leaves from the basil and put them into a blender or food processor with the feta, the remaining oil and 5ml/1 tsp salt. Blend until smooth, stir into the soup and simmer for a final 3 minutes. Serve immediately.

Energy 506kcal/2127kJ; Protein 38.1g; Carbohydrate 46.4g, of which sugars 9.3g; Fat 20g, of which saturates 6g; Cholesterol 76mg; Calcium 113mg; Fibre 6.6g; Sodium 380mg.

Fish and shellfish

With the fabulous array of seafood available in Peru it is no wonder that there are so many delicious recipes to prepare and cook the fruits of the sea.

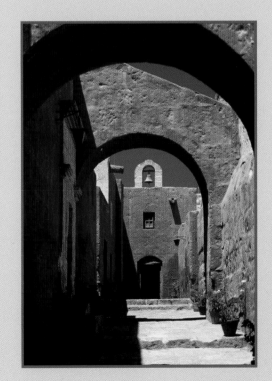

Exquisite fried fish or a sustaining chowder

Peru has 3,000 kilometres (1,865 miles) of coastline facing the South Pacific Ocean, along which two strong currents flow, the cold Humboldt current and the warm El Niño, and between them they control the coastal weather through the seasons. Their interaction also promotes the growth of plankton, the minuscule crustaceans that flourish in the Pacific Ocean and feed a vast wealth of fish and shellfish. In the north of Peru, close to the Equator, the catches are of tropical species, while cold-water species swim in the temperate waters to the south.

Some species of fish, such as the pejerrey (silverside), cojinova (palm ruff) and perico (parrotfish), are unique to the region. Peruvian mero, or sea bass, is sought after for its flavour and size, and the lenguado is a very large sole with exquisite white flesh. The writer Ernest Hemingway used to travel to Tumbes in the north to catch swordfish, a species prized by sport fishermen and still abundant. There are sea turtles, black scallops in the mangrove swamps, and the distinctive crayfish that inhabit the rivers flowing from the Andes down to the sea.

There are almost as many ways to prepare and eat fish and shellfish as there are species in Peru. Clams, scallops, cockles, sea urchins and more can be eaten straight from the sea just with lime juice and salt, while others such as whelks, octopus and limpets have to be boiled first, and are then enhanced with more elaborate sauces. Fish and shellfish go into a wide range of other Peruvian dishes, such as aguaditos (soup thickened with rice), escabeches (fried fish marinated in an oniony dressing), ajies (shellfish with hot chilli sauce), chicharrones (fried bitesize pieces of fish and shellfish) and picantes (stews with chilli and potatoes). Different recipes bring out the flavour of each type of fish.

Marinated steamed sea bass
Sudado de pescado

Serves 2

1 sea bass, weighing about
   500g/1¼lb, scaled
   and cleaned

2.5ml/½ tsp ground black
   pepper

2.5ml/½ tsp ground cumin

45ml/3 tbsp red wine vinegar

75ml/5 tbsp vegetable oil

1 large red onion, chopped

1 small tomato, chopped

1 small piece of red (bell)
   pepper, diced

1 chilli, seeded and finely
   chopped

15ml/1 tbsp grated garlic

10ml/2 tsp paprika

salt

boiled cassava and rice,
   to serve

This recipe comes from Tumbes, the region closest to the Equator with a tropical climate and wonderful seafood. Using an ancient technique, the fish is steamed with a little vinegar or chicha, the drink made from fermented corn.

1 Season the sea bass with pepper, cumin and salt. Pour the vinegar over it and leave to marinate for 15 minutes.

2 Heat the oil in a large frying pan and fry the onion for 5 minutes over medium heat. When it starts to brown, add the chopped tomato, diced pepper, chopped chilli, garlic and paprika and cook for a further 5 minutes.

3 Lay the fish in the pan and pour in its seasonings and vinegar. Cover the pan and leave the fish to steam for 15 minutes at medium heat.

4 Using a fork, carefully check that the fish is cooked: if the flesh flakes easily, remove from the heat. Serve the fish accompanied by boiled cassava and white rice.

Energy 592kcal/2471kJ; Protein 50.6g; Carbohydrate 27.8g, of which sugars 21.2g; Fat 31.8g, of which saturates 4g; Cholesterol 120mg; Calcium 77mg; Fibre 5.7g; Sodium 750mg.

Fried fish with onion and tomato sauce
Pescado a la chorrillana

A century ago Chorrillos was a fishing village to the south of Lima, but its beaches made it a very popular resort. Today it is a district of the city, but the fishing boats are still there, bringing their catch to the many kiosks that serve fried fish.

1 Season the fish with salt and pepper and dust with flour. Heat the oil in a frying pan, reserving 30ml/2 tbsp, and fry the fillets, turning once, until golden and cooked through. Transfer them to a plate and keep warm.

2 Heat the remaining oil over medium heat and fry the onions until they are browned. Add the garlic, tomatoes, chilli strips and chilli sauce and the oregano. Cook for 5 minutes.

3 Spoon the onion and tomato mixture into a serving dish and lay the fish on top, or transfer the sauce to a bowl and serve on the side. Sprinkle the fish with lime juice and garnish with parsley. Serve with rice or boiled potatoes.

Serves 6

6 white fish fillets, such as cod, haddock or sea bass

50g/2oz plain (all-purpose) flour

250ml/8fl oz/1 cup vegetable oil

3 medium red onions, sliced into rings

3 garlic cloves, finely chopped

4 medium tomatoes, peeled, seeded and diced

2 fresh chillies, seeded and thinly cut lengthways

15ml/1 tbsp chilli sauce

2.5ml/½ tsp dried oregano

juice of 1 lime

salt and ground black pepper

parsley leaves, to garnish

rice or boiled potatoes, to serve

Energy 412kcal/1712kJ; Protein 29.6g; Carbohydrate 14.6g, of which sugars 6.3g; Fat 26.5g, of which saturates 2.8g; Cholesterol 69mg; Calcium 50mg; Fibre 1.9g; Sodium 97mg.

Dry fish stew with coriander
Seco de pescado

A seco is a 'dry' style of stew that can be made with fish or meat. The recipe, from northern Peru, uses coriander and other locally grown ingredients. The cooking of the north includes many versions of seco made with chicken, kid and lamb.

1 Arrange the fish fillets in a wide pan and cover with the slices of onion and red pepper.

2 Put the garlic, ginger, coriander, cumin, chilli sauce and oil into a blender or food processor and blend to a purée. Spoon over the fish and leave to marinate for 15 minutes.

3 Put the pan on a high heat until the fish is starting to sizzle, pour in the beer and add the peas and bring to the boil. Reduce the heat, cover the pan and simmer for 15 minutes.

4 When the fish is cooked, squeeze the lime juice over the top, and serve with rice.

Serves 6

6 white fish fillets, such as cod or swordfish

1 large red onion, sliced lengthways

1 red (bell) pepper, thinly sliced

3 garlic cloves

2.5cm/1in piece fresh root ginger

100g/3¾oz fresh coriander (cilantro)

1.5ml/¼ tsp ground cumin

45ml/3 tbsp chilli sauce

120ml/4fl oz/½ cup vegetable oil

120ml/4fl oz/½ cup white beer

250g/9oz/2 cups shelled peas

juice of 1 lime

salt and ground black pepper

boiled rice, to serve

Energy 302kcal/1257kJ; Protein 31.5g; Carbohydrate 9.6g, of which sugars 5.4g; Fat 14.9g, of which saturates 1.6g; Cholesterol 69mg; Calcium 63mg; Fibre 3.5g; Sodium 183mg.

Corn purée with fried fish
Espesado norteno con pescado frito

Serves 4

4 fresh corn cobs

500ml/17fl oz/generous 2 cups water

25g/1oz fresh coriander (cilantro)

150ml/5fl oz/⅔ cup vegetable oil

1 medium red onion, finely chopped

2 chicken or vegetable stock (bouillon) cubes

1.5ml/¼ tsp ground cumin

10ml/2 tsp chilli sauce

4 fish fillets, such as mahi mahi or halibut

40g/1½oz plain (all-purpose) flour

salt and ground black pepper

lime halves, to serve

Peruvian corn was developed in the age of the Incas, or maybe even earlier. There are two basic kinds: one from the coast, which has a large white kernel with a bland flavour, and one from the mountains, which is sweeter and crisper. This recipe can be made with the kind of fresh corn on the cob that is available everywhere.

1 Slice the kernels off the corn cobs and blend them with half the water in a blender or food processor. Transfer to a bowl and set aside.

2 Put the coriander in the blender with half the remaining water, and blend to a purée.

3 Heat 30ml/2 tbsp of the oil in a deep pan and fry the onion until golden. Add the stock cubes, cumin, chilli sauce and the remaining water. Stir until the stock cubes have dissolved.

4 Add the blended corn kernels and simmer for 5–10 minutes, stirring constantly to avoid the mixture sticking. Stir in the coriander purée and cook for 1 minute, then remove from the heat. Pour into a serving dish and keep warm.

5 Season the fish fillets with salt and pepper and dust them with flour. Fry them in the remaining oil, turning once, until golden on both sides and cooked through. Serve immediately with the corn purée and half a lime.

Energy 508kcal/2122kJ; Protein 31.7g; Carbohydrate 35.3g, of which sugars 10.6g; Fat 27.5g, of which saturates 3g; Cholesterol 69mg; Calcium 57mg; Fibre 2.4g; Sodium 393mg.

Fried fish with shellfish sauce
Pescado a lo macho

The historic port of Callao has been full of culinary treasures since the 16th century, when it was the region's centre of trade. Laden mules from Bolivia and Argentina carried goods over the Andes to Callao, which were then shipped to Spain. This dish is typical of Callao's famous seafood recipes.

1 Scrub and clean the mussels, discarding any that are open and fail to close when tapped sharply, and put them in a pan with a little water. Bring to the boil over a high heat, cover, and cook until opened. Drain, discarding any that fail to open after about 5 minutes. Using a teaspoon, detach the flesh from the shells. Discard the shells.

2 Steam and shell the cockles and clams in the same way. Clean and slice the squid, peel and devein the prawns and slice the scallops.

3 Season the fish fillets with salt and pepper and dust with flour. Heat the oil in a frying pan, reserving 30–45ml/2–3 tbsp, and fry the fillets over a high heat, turning once, until golden and cooked through. Transfer them to a serving dish and keep warm.

4 Heat the remaining oil in a large pan over medium heat and fry the onion for about 10 minutes, until golden brown. Stir in the chilli sauce, paprika and cumin and season well with salt and pepper.

5 Add all the prepared shellfish to the pan and cook, stirring, for 2 minutes, then add the wine, cover the pan and simmer for 5 minutes.

6 Pour the seafood sauce over the fried fish and serve immediately, accompanied by rice or boiled potatoes.

Cook's tip When dishes are highly flavoured like this one, Peruvians normally accompany them with plain rice or boiled potatoes to emphasize the flavours of the ingredients and make them more digestible.

Serves 6

12 mussels

12 cockles

12 clams

6 small squid

12 king prawns (jumbo shrimp)

12 scallops

6 white fish fillets, such as sea bass, haddock or sole

50g/2oz plain (all-purpose) flour

250ml/8fl oz/1 cup vegetable oil

1 large red onion, diced

15ml/1 tbsp chilli sauce

5ml/1 tsp paprika

2.5ml/½ tsp ground cumin

1 glass white wine

salt and ground black pepper

boiled potatoes or rice, to serve

Energy 343kcal/1429kJ; Protein 31.1g; Carbohydrate 9.1g, of which sugars 0.9g; Fat 18.4g, of which saturates 2g; Cholesterol 133mg; Calcium 86mg; Fibre 0.4g; Sodium 668mg.

Mussels in chilli sauce
Aji de choros

Eating mussels is a must in the Peruvian capital, Lima, where they are plentiful on the nearby beaches, attached to the large rocks. Here they are cooked in an aji, a tasty dish that takes its name from the Peruvian chilli that is its key ingredient. Use large frozen mussels if you can't find fresh.

Serves 6

1kg/2¼lb New Zealand greenshell mussels, fresh or frozen

100g/3¾oz shelled walnuts

350ml/12fl oz evaporated milk

12 slices white bread, reduced to crumbs

75ml/5 tbsp vegetable oil

1 large red onion, finely chopped

4 garlic cloves, crushed

45ml/3 tbsp chilli sauce

5ml/1 tsp ground turmeric

2.5ml/½ tsp ground black pepper

15ml/1 tbsp chopped parsley, to garnish

1 hard-boiled egg, sliced, to garnish

rice and peas or boiled potatoes, to serve

1 If using fresh whole mussels, scrub them, and remove the beards. Discard any that are open and fail to close when tapped sharply. Place the mussels in a large pan with 2 litres/3½ pints/8 cups water. Bring to the boil then reduce the heat and simmer for 20 minutes. Drain, reserving the stock, and discarding any mussels that do not open.

2 Remove all but 12 mussels from their shells, and keep warm. Do the same if using frozen mussels. At this point some Peruvian cooks would remove the dark part with a teaspoon.

3 Put the walnuts in a blender or food processor with a little of the evaporated milk and grind to a purée. Soak the breadcrumbs in the rest of the milk for 15 minutes.

4 Heat the oil in a large pan and fry the onion and garlic for 10 minutes, until caramelized. Add the chilli sauce, turmeric and pepper.

5 Add the bread and milk mixture and 500ml/17fl oz/generous 2 cups of the reserved stock to the pan. Simmer for 10

minutes, stirring constantly to avoid the mixture sticking to the base of the pan.

6 Stir in the shelled mussels and the puréed walnuts and simmer for 5 minutes.

7 Turn into a serving dish and garnish with the mussels in their shells, chopped parsley and hard-boiled egg. Serve accompanied by rice and peas or boiled potatoes.

Energy 437kcal/1831kJ; Protein 20.7g; Carbohydrate 34.3g, of which sugars 8.5g; Fat 25.2g, of which saturates 3.8g; Cholesterol 30mg; Calcium 331mg; Fibre 1.5g; Sodium 455mg.

Whelks and potatoes in red chilli sauce
Guiso de caracoles de mar

Serves 4

75ml/5 tbsp vegetable oil

1 large red onion, finely chopped

15ml/1 tbsp chilli sauce

500g/1¼lb white potatoes, peeled and cut into 2cm/¾in dice

2 fish or vegetable stock (bouillon) cubes dissolved in 500ml/17fl oz/generous 2 cups water

500g/1¼lb cooked whelks, cut into 1cm/½in pieces

salt

15ml/1 tbsp chopped parsley, to garnish

boiled rice and corn on the cob, to serve

The South Pacific produces a wealth of shellfish, and local cooks have devised many recipes. One of these is the picante, a spicy stew of shellfish and potatoes. It is often very hot, but in here the amount of chilli is subtle.

1 Heat the oil and fry the onion over high heat for 3 minutes, then reduce the heat to medium and cook for a further 7 minutes, until starting to brown. Stir in the chilli sauce.

2 Add the potatoes and the stock to the pan, bring to the boil and cook for 20 minutes.

3 Add the whelks, season with salt if necessary (the stock may be salty enough) and simmer for a further 5 minutes, until the potatoes are tender and the whelks are heated through.

4 Transfer to a serving dish, sprinkle with parsley and serve with rice and corn.

Energy 362kcal/1514kJ; Protein 27.9g; Carbohydrate 28.2g, of which sugars 7.3g; Fat 16g, of which saturates 1.8g; Cholesterol 156mg; Calcium 138mg; Fibre 2.7g; Sodium 577mg.

Crayfish and potato stew with fresh cheese
Cauche de camarones

The Peruvian variety of crayfish proliferate in the rivers of the south and there is no greater delicacy than fresh crayfish straight out of the water. The evaporated milk adds a touch of sweetness as well as a creamy texture.

1 Pour 350ml/12fl oz/1½ cups water into a large pan and bring to a boil. Drop the crayfish or prawns in, cover, and cook for 10 minutes.

2 Strain and reserve the stock: there should be about 250ml/8fl oz/1 cup. Put aside six whole crayfish or prawns. Peel the rest, remove their heads, and devein.

3 Boil the potatoes in their skins in lightly salted water until tender, then peel them and cut into 1cm/½in slices.

4 Heat the butter in a large pan and cook the onion until softened. Stir in the chilli sauce, paprika, tomatoes and mint, and cook for 3 minutes. Add the crayfish or prawn tails, the reserved stock, cheese and sliced potatoes.

5 Bring to the boil and simmer for 5 minutes, or until the cheese has melted. Add the evaporated milk, season to taste with salt and simmer for 5 more minutes. Serve, garnished with chopped parsley or mint leaves and the reserved whole crayfish or prawns.

Serves 6

675g/1½lb raw crayfish or king prawns (jumbo shrimp)

1kg/2¼lb floury potatoes

75ml/5 tbsp butter

1 small red onion, finely chopped

60ml/4 tbsp chilli sauce

5ml/1 tsp paprika

3 medium tomatoes, peeled, seeded and diced

5ml/1 tsp black mint (peppermint) leaves, finely sliced

500g/1¼lb queso fresco or mild feta cheese, cut into 2cm/¾in dice

120ml/4fl oz/½ cup evaporated milk

15ml/1 tbsp chopped parsley or mint leaves, to garnish

salt

Energy 541kcal/2262kJ; Protein 36.6g; Carbohydrate 34.1g, of which sugars 9.3g; Fat 29.5g, of which saturates 19g; Cholesterol 222mg; Calcium 411mg; Fibre 2.3g; Sodium 1639mg.

Fried seafood platter
Jalea de mariscos

Peruvians are very keen on dishes of bitesize, crispy fried morsels. They are normally called chicharrones, and although usually made of pork, chicken, fish or shellfish can also be prepared this way. This dish is normally accompanied by fried cassava and onion salsa, and is served on a single dish or platter for everyone to help themselves.

1 If using fresh mussels, scrub and remove the beard. Discard any that remain open when tapped. Clean and slice the squid. Steam open the clams and scallops in a little boiling water, and remove the meat from the shells. Cut the dark part of the mussel away if you wish. Peel the king prawn tails.

2 Boil the cassava for 20 minutes in lightly salted water, then drain and dry with a clean dish towel. Season with salt and pepper.

3 Mix the sliced onions with the lime juice, chilli and parsley and set aside.

4 Heat some of the oil in a large frying pan and fry the pieces of cassava until they are golden on all sides. Transfer them to a serving dish or platter and keep warm.

5 Season the pieces of fish and dust with cornflour. Fry the fish in the remaining oil over medium-high heat for 2–3 minutes, turning, until it is an even golden brown colour. Remove from the pan with a slotted spoon and drain thoroughly on kitchen paper, then arrange over the fried cassava and keep warm.

6 Repeat with each type of seafood, frying it in small batches over a high heat so that it cooks very quickly without becoming tough. Remove each batch and drain on kitchen paper, then arrange on the dish with the fish.

7 When all the seafood is prepared, sprinkle the onions and lime juice on top. Place the dish on the table for everyone to help themselves.

Serves 4

- 12 New Zealand greenshell mussels, fresh or frozen
- 12 small squid
- 12 clams
- 6 scallops
- 12 raw king prawn (jumbo shrimp) tails
- 500g/1¼lb cassava, cut into chunks
- 2 medium red onions, finely sliced lengthways
- juice of 2 limes
- 1 fresh chilli, sliced
- 30ml/2 tbsp chopped parsley
- 250ml/8fl oz/1 cup vegetable oil
- 500g/1¼lb firm-fleshed white fish, such as mahi mahi, cut into 2.5cm/1in chunks
- 250g/9oz/2 cups cornflour (corn starch)
- salt and ground black pepper

Energy 747kcal/3141kJ; Protein 41.8g; Carbohydrate 86.7g, of which sugars 7.4g; Fat 28.2g, of which saturates 3.3g; Cholesterol 153mg; Calcium 114mg; Fibre 3.7g; Sodium 607mg.

Seafood rice
Arroz con mariscos

This rice dish mixes elements of classical Spanish cuisine with the abundant seafood of the South Pacific. It is the Peruvian interpretation of the traditional paella, adapted to Peruvian ingredients and flavourings.

1 Clean the clams, discard any that remain open when tapped. Slice the bodies of the squid and leave the tentacles whole.

2 Heat the oil in a large frying pan over medium heat and fry the onion with the garlic for 10 minutes, until browned. Add the paprika and season with salt and pepper.

3 Pour in the wine and fish stock, raise the heat to high and cook the crab claws for 8 minutes.

4 Add the whelks, squid and clams and cook for a further 7 minutes. Then add the mussels, if fresh, and cook for another 5 minutes, then the scallops and peas and cook for another 3 minutes, reducing the heat to medium.

5 When all clam shells have opened, add the cooked rice and stir for a further 2 minutes until it is mixed in and heated through. Add the diced pepper and the sliced chilli. Sprinkle with chopped parsley before serving.

Serves 4

150g/5oz clams

150g/5oz squid

120ml/4fl oz/½ cup olive oil

1 large red onion, chopped

5 garlic cloves, finely chopped

15ml/1 tbsp paprika

250ml/8fl oz/1 cup white wine

250ml/8fl oz/1 cup fish stock

4 crab claws

200g/7oz whelks

200g/7oz New Zealand
  greenshell mussels

200g/7oz scallops

250g/9oz/2 cups shelled peas

675g/1½lb/3 cups cooked rice

1 red (bell) pepper, diced

1 chilli, seeded and finely
  sliced

salt and ground black pepper

fresh parsley, chopped,
  to garnish

Energy 714kcal/2997kJ; Protein 48.9g; Carbohydrate 65.3g, of which sugars 4.5g; Fat 26g, of which saturates 4.1g; Cholesterol 213mg; Calcium 177mg; Fibre 3.8g; Sodium 832mg.

Spicy seafood stew
Picante de mariscos

Serves 6

500g/1¼lb floury potatoes,

75ml/5 tbsp vegetable oil

1 medium red onion, finely chopped

3 garlic cloves, finely chopped

30ml/2 tbsp chilli sauce

250ml/8fl oz/1 cup dry white wine or light beer

1kg/2¼lb mixed seafood: mussels, whelks, scallops, squid, king prawns (jumbo shrimp), etc, cleaned

30ml/2 tbsp potato flour (starch) or cornflour (cornstarch)

salt and ground black pepper

Most Peruvian stews containing chilli and potatoes have their origins in the south of the country. However, that does not mean they are exclusively prepared in that region. This traditional dish is found in every seafood restaurant throughout the country. It is most often accompanied by boiled rice.

1 Boil the potatoes in their skins in salted water for 20 minutes, until tender. Drain and peel. Cut into slices and keep warm in a serving dish.

2 While the potatoes are cooking, heat the oil in a large pan and fry the onion and garlic for 10 minutes until the onion is golden. Add the chilli sauce, pour in the wine or beer and simmer for about 15 minutes.

3 Add the seafood mixture to the pan and season with salt and pepper. Simmer for a further 5 minutes.

4 Slake the potato flour or cornflour in 45ml/ 3 tbsp cold water and add to the stew. Simmer, stirring constantly. As soon as it thickens, remove from the heat and pour the sauce over the potato slices. Serve immediately.

Energy 335kcal/1405kJ; Protein 32g; Carbohydrate 22.7g, of which sugars 5.4g; Fat 10.6g, of which saturates 1.2g; Cholesterol 325mg; Calcium 161mg; Fibre 1.7g; Sodium 385mg.

Meat, game and poultry

Although Peruvians love their fish and vegetables, meat is central to their cuisine, with many of the national dishes using it as the main ingredient.

Regional favourites and national dishes

Peruvians love meat, and the climate gives the farmers scope to raise a wide variety of livestock. Although the Incas were not great meat-eaters, they used to eat llama meat, either fresh or dried, and hunted some of the indigenous wild animals for food. The arrival of the Spanish brought poultry, sheep, cattle and pigs to the farms of Peru, all of which were easily incorporated into the traditional cuisine, and most Peruvians these days have inherited a love of meat from their Spanish forebears.

The far greater range of game available in the rainforest also found its way into the Spanish colonials' kitchens. Animals such as red deer, capybara, peccary, tapir, agouti and armadillo all became part of the culinary repertoire.

Whether the meat is game or not, there are never any leftovers; the carcass will be almost totally consumed. Peruvians like to use everything up, because they feel that waste is simply not an option, and that it disturbs cosmic harmony. The earth and its products are gifts and must be treated as such, not partly used and then rejected, so although they love the best cuts such as a simple steak, Peruvians will eat every part of an animal, including the tongue, heart and intestines. They make many delicious dishes from the offal and other cuts that might be spurned in other countries, including 'cau cau' with tripe, flavoured with turmeric; 'patita con mani', a stew made of pig's and cow's feet; and even chicken gizzards 'Trujillo style', cooked to perfection with herbs and spices.

As Peru is a very large country, there are noticeable regional differences in the cuisine, especially in meat recipes, where the ingredients might not be available country-wide. The name 'seco' is given to a dry stew flavoured with coriander that is often made with goat in the north, beef in the central coastal regions and lamb in the south.

Stir-fried beef fillet with fried potatoes
Lomo saltado

Serves 4

500g/1¼lb beef fillet

475ml/16fl oz/2 cup
  vegetable oil

5ml/1 tsp dried oregano

1 medium onion, sliced

1 beefsteak tomato, chopped

1 fresh red chilli, seeded and
  sliced

500g/1¼lb potatoes, peeled
  and cut into chips (fries)

salt and ground black pepper

5ml/1 tsp parsley, chopped,
  to garnish

chilli relish (see Cook's tip)

A sauté of onion, garlic and tomato is the starting point for many Peruvian dishes, and it sometimes also provides the final garnish. In this recipe, tender beef is given a topping of this mixture, together with fried potatoes. As usual with dishes from the coastal region, it is traditionally accompanied by plain rice or rice and peas.

1 Cut the beef into 2cm/¾in cubes. Heat 60ml/4 tbsp of the oil over a high heat and stir-fry the meat quickly until it is brown on all sides. Remove to a serving dish, season with salt, pepper and oregano and keep warm.

2 Heat another 60ml/4 tbsp of oil and fry the onion for about 4 minutes, until browned, then add the tomato and the chilli and cook until the tomato releases its juice. Season and spoon the mixture on top of the beef.

3 Heat the remaining oil in a clean frying pan and fry the potatoes for about 10 minutes, or until golden. Drain and arrange on top of the stir-fried beef. Garnish with parsley and serve immediately with chilli relish.

Cook's tip To make a chilli relish to serve with the beef, put 3 green or red chillies, seeded, into a blender with 200g/7oz feta cheese, 100g/3¾oz parsley leaves, 45ml/3 tbsp olive oil and salt to taste, and blend together.

Energy 558kcal/2321kJ; Protein 31.5g; Carbohydrate 25.6g, of which sugars 6g; Fat 37.2g, of which saturates 7.5g; Cholesterol 73mg; Calcium 30mg; Fibre 2.5g; Sodium 100mg.

Beef stew with carrots and potatoes
Estofado de carne

This casserole is similar to many found throughout the world, but also very Peruvian. Many Peruvians consider it to be especially characteristic of Cuzco, but the dish actually has its roots in several Peruvian cities, especially those that had a substantial Spanish population after the conquest. Almost as soon as the Spanish began to cook with tomatoes, this combination of ingredients was developed. Estofado is usually served with plain rice.

1 Cut the beef into 4cm/1½in cubes. Heat the oil in a large pan and fry the beef quickly, turning, until browned on all sides. Remove the beef from the pan and set aside.

2 Reduce the heat to medium-high. Add the onion and fry until golden. Return the beef to the pan and add the chopped tomato.

3 Add the remaining ingredients and season with salt. Bring to the boil, cover and simmer for 30 minutes, or until the meat is tender. Serve.

Cook's tip If you use a cheaper cut of beef, such as braising (stewing) steak, increase the cooking time to 1 hour. This stew can also be made using chicken instead of beef.

Serves 4

500g/1¼lb rump (round) steak

90ml/6 tbsp vegetable oil

1 large onion, diced

1 large tomato, chopped

500g/1¼lb potatoes, peeled and halved

250g/9oz carrots, peeled and cut in batons

250g/9oz/2 cups shelled peas

250ml/8fl oz/1 cup passata (bottled strained tomatoes)

2 bay leaves

1 litre/1¾ pints/4 cups water

salt

Energy 582kcal/2426kJ; Protein 37.3g; Carbohydrate 43.5g, of which sugars 16.7g; Fat 30g, of which saturates 6.9g; Cholesterol 73mg; Calcium 77mg; Fibre 8g; Sodium 261mg.

Tripe and potato stew
Cau cau

It is sometimes said that this dish comes from African slaves in Peru, who ate the innards of animals because that is all they were given, but the Spanish loved offal too, and although turmeric in this recipe does show a North African influence, it is also one of the 20 spices used in Peru before the Spanish conquest.

1 Put the tripe in a pan with the mint sprigs and 1 litre/1¾ pints/4 cups of the water. Bring to the boil and cook, covered, for 20 minutes. Drain, and cut the tripe into 1cm/½in squares.

2 Heat the oil over medium-high heat and fry the onion for 10 minutes until browned, then add the chilli sauce and the turmeric. Stir well and add the remaining water, the potatoes and the prepared tripe. Season with salt.

3 Bring to the boil and leave to simmer, covered, for 25–30 minutes, until the potatoes are tender. Add the chopped parsley and serve as it is, or with sweet potatoes.

Cook's tip Make this chilli sauce to serve with the stew. Blend together 3 large red chillies, seeded, with 2 garlic cloves, a splash of oil, a small onion, sliced and fried, and a good seasoning of salt.

Serves 4

500g/1¼lb cooked beef tripe

2–3 sprigs mint

1.5 litres/2½ pints/6 cups water

60ml/4 tbsp vegetable oil

1 medium onion, chopped

15ml/1 tbsp chilli sauce

15ml/1 tbsp ground turmeric

500g/1¼lb potatoes, peeled and cut into small chunks

15ml/1 tbsp chopped parsley

salt

Energy 272kcal/1138kJ; Protein 14.4g; Carbohydrate 22.3g, of which sugars 3.4g; Fat 14.5g, of which saturates 2.7g; Cholesterol 119mg; Calcium 109mg; Fibre 1.7g; Sodium 90mg.

Lamb stew with boiled cassava
Seco de cordero

Serves 4

500g/1¼lb boneless lamb leg steaks

90ml/6 tbsp vegetable oil

1 medium onion, finely chopped

5ml/1 tsp ground cumin

15ml/1 tbsp chilli sauce

1 bunch coriander (cilantro)

1 litre/1¾ pints/4 cups water

500g/1¼lb white potatoes, peeled and halved

500g/1¼lb cassava, peeled and cut into 7.5cm/3in chunks

250g/9oz/2 cups shelled peas

salt

white rice (see page 103) and chilli sauce (see page 84), to serve

Stews are very much part of the Peruvian kitchen, as home cooks enjoy following recipes and appreciate a clever combination of ingredients. This kind of stew, called seco (dry) to distinguish it from the soupy aguadito, contains potatoes, cassava, coriander, chilli and spices. It is served with rice and often with beans too, and with chilli sauce on the table for those who like extra heat.

1 Cut the meat into 5cm/2in pieces. Heat the oil in a large pan and fry the meat over medium to high heat until browned on all sides. Reduce the heat, add the onion and fry until it is golden, then add the cumin and chilli sauce.

2 Purée the coriander in a blender or processor with 250ml/8fl oz/1 cup of the water.

3 Add the coriander paste to the pan with the remaining water and bring to the boil, then add the potatoes, cassava and peas. Season.

4 Cover the pan and leave to simmer for 30 minutes, or until the meat and vegetables are tender. Serve immediately with white rice and chilli sauce.

Energy 662kcal/2771kJ; Protein 34.2g; Carbohydrate 62.1g, of which sugars 16.1g; Fat 32.6g, of which saturates 8.7g; Cholesterol 95mg; Calcium 113mg; Fibre 9.2g; Sodium 180mg.

Hen and potatoes in chilli sauce
Aji de gallina

What happens to a hen when it stops laying eggs? Normally, in Peru, it is killed and eaten, but its meat is tough because of its age, so it needs to be prepared in a way that will tenderize the meat. This recipe, with Spanish origins adapted to the Peruvian style, does just that and has remained in the repertoire for centuries, but the method is the basis of many similar dishes, using a variety of meat or fish. In all of them the essential ingredient in the sauce is chilli. This version is made with a roasting chicken, which is readily available, rather than a hen, but the name has been kept.

Serves 6

1 small chicken weighing about 1.2kg/2½lb, jointed

1 large carrot, peeled

1 celery heart

1 thin leek

2 litres/3½ pints/8 cups water

salt

For the chilli sauce:

3 red chillies, seeded and roughly chopped

6 medium slices white bread, reduced to crumbs

175ml/6fl oz/¾ cup evaporated milk

90ml/6 tbsp vegetable oil

1 medium onion, finely chopped

50g/2oz/½ cup ground almonds

50g/2oz/⅔ cup grated Parmesan cheese

To serve:

6 portions white rice

6 lettuce leaves

500g/1¼lb King Edward potatoes, boiled in their skins, then peeled

6 kalamata olives, pitted

3 hard-boiled eggs

chilli strips (optional)

1 Place the chicken in a pan with the carrot, celery and leek. Pour in the water and season with salt. Bring to the boil and skim, then simmer, covered, for 40 minutes.

2 Lift out the chicken and strain and reserve the stock. Strip the chicken flesh from the bones and shred it very finely. Set aside.

3 To make the chilli sauce, put the chillies in a blender or food processor with 100ml/3½fl oz/scant ½ cup water and blend to a purée. Set aside.

4 Soak the breadcrumbs in the evaporated milk for 5 minutes, blend the mixture to a smooth paste and set aside.

5 Heat the oil in a large pan and fry the onion for 10 minutes, stirring, until it browns. Add the chilli purée and cook for 3 minutes. Add the bread and milk mixture and stir until it thickens.

6 Stir the shredded chicken into the sauce, and add 750ml/1¼ pints/3 cups of the reserved stock. Continue to cook, stirring, until the sauce is hot and the consistency is creamy and smooth.

7 Add the ground almonds and the Parmesan cheese and simmer for 5 more minutes.

8 Slice the boiled, peeled potatoes, and shell and halve the hard-boiled eggs.

9 To assemble the dish, begin by arranging a portion of rice (or rice with corn) on each plate. Place a lettuce leaf beside the rice. Place three slices of potato on top of each lettuce leaf.

10 Spoon some of the chicken mixture on top of the potatoes and, to finish, garnish with an olive and half a hard-boiled egg. Add a few strips of chilli, if you wish.

Energy 495kcal/2062kJ; Protein 34.7g; Carbohydrate 20.9g, of which sugars 6.9g; Fat 30.8g, of which saturates 9.1g; Cholesterol 141mg; Calcium 249mg; Fibre 1.6g; Sodium 368mg.

Rabbit in peanut sauce
Conejo en salsa de mani

Serves 4

4 rabbit leg joints

250ml/8fl oz/1 cup red wine vinegar

2 rosemary sprigs

10ml/2 tsp ground paprika

4 garlic cloves, crushed

2.5ml/½ tsp ground black pepper

60ml/4 tbsp vegetable oil

250ml/8fl oz/1 cup white wine

250ml/8fl oz/1 cup water

1 quince or large cooking apple, peeled and sliced

200g/7oz/1¾ cups roasted, salted peanuts, ground in a blender

salt

There were wild rabbits in the Americas before the Spanish arrived, but that population was added to by escaped rabbits brought as food. After escaping they multiplied so much that they populated the whole region, so for five centuries they have been eaten by Peruvians. A good way to enjoy rabbit is deep-fried (chicharrones de conejo), but it is normally eaten roasted, or in stews like this one.

1 Put the rabbit joints in a bowl with the vinegar, rosemary, paprika, garlic, black pepper and salt and leave to marinate for 2 hours.

2 Heat the oil over high heat. Dry the pieces of rabbit and fry on each side, until browned.

3 Add the wine and the water to the pan together with the slices of quince or apple and the peanuts. Bring to the boil then reduce the heat to medium, cover the pan and simmer for 30 minutes, until the rabbit is tender. Serve the rabbit with rice or boiled potatoes.

Energy 559kcal/2324kJ; Protein 35.2g; Carbohydrate 9g, of which sugars 5g; Fat 38.3g, of which saturates 6.9g; Cholesterol 71mg; Calcium 63mg; Fibre 3.4g; Sodium 72mg.

Turkey and corn stew
Pepian de pavo

Turkey is a very popular meat in the north of Peru. Many households and most farms still rear their own birds, so the region has many recipes that use the meat. The cooking techniques vary depending on the age at which the turkeys are killed. Normally a dish like this, which quickly fries the meat, would be prepared with the tender breast meat from a young female bird.

1 Using a sharp knife, strip the kernels from the corn on the cob. Put them in batches in a blender or food processor and blend to a paste.

2 Heat the oil in a large pan and fry the turkey over a high heat for 8–10 minutes, until golden on all sides. Stir in the onion and garlic, reduce the heat slightly and cook until the onion is caramelized.

3 Add the chilli purée and cook for 3 minutes, then pour in the chicken stock. Bring to the boil and simmer for 20 minutes. Season to taste with salt.

4 Add the puréed corn and simmer for a further 15 minutes, until thick. Garnish with parsley and serve the turkey stew with white rice.

Serves 4

6 corn cobs

90ml/6 tbsp vegetable oil

500g/1¼lb skinless turkey breast fillet, cut into 2cm/¾in cubes

1 medium onion, finely chopped

2 garlic cloves, sliced or crushed

2 red chillies, seeded, blended to a purée in 60ml/4 tbsp water

500ml/17fl oz/generous 2 cups chicken stock

salt

chopped parsley, to garnish

white rice (see page 103), to serve

Energy 472kcal/1980kJ; Protein 34g; Carbohydrate 42g, of which sugars 15.9g; Fat 19.8g, of which saturates 2.4g; Cholesterol 61mg; Calcium 24mg; Fibre 2.5g; Sodium 461mg.

Duck with rice
Arroz con pato

When rice first arrived in Peru with the Spanish it was a great delicacy, and even though it is now a daily staple it is no less valued. Peruvians truly enjoy rice simply cooked with garlic and oil, but also like to use it to absorb flavours and cooking liquids as in this dish. This classic recipe for duck with rice comes from the north coast, especially the regions of La Libertad, Lambayeque and Piura. The best accompaniment is a very cold beer, though Peruvians also drink chicha de jora with this.

1 Pierce the skin of the duck all over with a fork, wash and dry with kitchen paper.

2 Put the coriander leaves in a blender or food processor with 500ml/17fl oz/generous 2 cups water and blend to a purée.

3 Heat a little oil in a large pan and, when very hot, fry the duck pieces, moving them around until browned on all sides. Remove from the pan and set aside on a plate.

4 Reduce the heat to medium, add the onion and garlic to the pan and fry until softened and golden brown.

5 Return the duck to the pan with the coriander purée and sliced peppers. Season with salt and cumin and pour in 500ml/17fl oz/generous 2 cups water.

6 Increase the heat and bring to the boil, place the whole yellow chilli on top, reduce the heat and simmer, covered, for 20 minutes.

7 When the duck is cooked, add the pisco or beer, peas and rice. Keep the heat at medium-high for 15 minutes, until the rice is partially cooked, then remove and reserve the whole chilli. Reduce the heat, stir the rice gently and simmer on a low heat, covered, for a further 10 minutes until the liquid is absorbed.

8 Serve immediately, dividing the duck portions among the diners and offering the cooked chilli to those who want extra heat.

Cook's tips The yellow chilli is a Peruvian speciality. If you cannot find it, you can add a mild chilli (such as a large red one), keeping it intact. If it is cut up it will make the whole dish hot, but if kept whole it will release flavour rather than heat. Those who want more heat can add it to their plate at the table.

If you are using beer you must allow the liquid to reduce at a rapid boil before adding the rice. The volume of liquid needs to be the same as that of rice, so it is all absorbed, too much liquid will spoil the dish.

Serves 4

1kg/2¼lb duck leg joints

large bunch fresh coriander (cilantro)

vegetable oil, for frying

1 medium onion, finely chopped

2 garlic cloves, crushed or sliced

2 medium red (bell) peppers, sliced

5ml/1 tsp ground cumin

1 whole yellow chilli (see Cook's tips)

60ml/4 tbsp pisco or 500ml/17fl oz/generous 2 cups beer (see Cook's tips)

250g/9oz/2 cups shelled peas

500g/1¼lb American long grain rice

salt

Energy 981kcal/4083kJ; Protein 33.2g; Carbohydrate 116.9g, of which sugars 10.5g; Fat 39.1g, of which saturates 7.9g; Cholesterol 75mg; Calcium 72mg; Fibre 4.6g; Sodium 122mg.

Vegetarian dishes and accompaniments

Peru's variety of vegetables is the most defining element of its cuisine, and the importance of food such as corn and the potato is rooted in the country's culture.

Rich in flavour, goodness and variety

Everyone knows nowadays that vegetables are rich in nutrients and essential to health, but a colourful array of vegetable dishes has always been part of the Peruvian way of life. In recent years, however, it has been discovered that some age-old practices really do have health benefits, such as the antioxidant properties of garlic, which is used in many recipes.

By including beans and grains alongside the vegetables, it is possible to eat a good, varied diet without having recourse to meat. A huge choice of vegetables is always available in Lima and other cities where the markets have access to produce grown throughout Peru, provided it can be transported by road. There are also many wonderful vegetables from the rainforest, but these are only available within the local area.

The produce on offer is varied and abundant. There are tubers such as potatoes, sweet potatoes and ollucos, and roots such as ocas, maca and cassava that have to be cooked, while others such as mooli (daikon), radishes, beetroots (beets) and carrots can also be eaten raw. The most widely used vegetables include corn on the cob, broad (fava) beans, onions, squash, and species unique to the Andes, such as the cucumber-like caigua. Sweet red (bell) peppers deserve a special mention, as they are essential ingredients in many recipes dating from pre-Inca times. Last but not least are the herbs used as flavourings.

But if there is a single product that represents Peru, it is the chilli pepper. Some 35 species of the genus Capsicum were first found in the Andes, and there are now more than 300 different species worldwide. This small fiery vegetable quite simply dominates Peruvian cuisine and lends its inimitable hot flavour to many dishes.

Swiss chard pie
Pastel de acelgas

Bakeries in Peru start selling Swiss chard pies at mid-morning. Eaten warm and fresh, they are simply delicious, and choosing between these pies and the empanadas with different fillings is difficult, as all of them are good. Use the filling for this pie to make little empanaditas if you wish.

1 To make the filling, blanch the Swiss chard in boiling water for 5 minutes then drain well and set aside.

2 Heat the oil in a pan over medium heat and fry the onion and garlic for 5 minutes until softened and starting to brown. Stir in the Swiss chard, nutmeg, salt and pepper and continue to cook for 3 minutes, then remove from the heat and leave to cool.

3 To make the pastry, sift the flour and salt into a bowl, then rub in the margarine using your fingers or two forks. Add the water and draw the pastry together with your fingers. Knead lightly to form a smooth dough and leave to rest in a cool place for 10 minutes.

4 Preheat the oven to 180°C/350°F/Gas 4 and oil a rectangular baking tray, 25x15cm/10x6in. Divide the dough into two pieces, one larger than the other.

5 On a floured surface, thinly roll out the larger piece of pastry and use to line the tray, leaving the edges of the pastry hanging over the sides.

6 Beat the eggs lightly together and stir them into the cooled filling. Pour the mixture into the pastry-lined tray. Cut the hard-boiled eggs in half and press them into the filling, distributing them evenly. Dampen the edges of the pastry.

7 Roll out the remaining dough and cover the pie, sealing the edges by pressing them together with your fingers. Trim the edges and cut out decorations for the top from the pastry trimmings if you wish.

8 Brush the surface of the pie with the egg yolk and bake for about 45 minutes until the pastry is crisp and golden brown. Leave to cool before slicing and serving as an appetizer.

Serves 8

For the filling:

1kg/2¼lb Swiss chard, thickly sliced

45ml/3 tbsp vegetable oil

1 small red onion, finely chopped

2 garlic cloves, chopped

2.5ml/½ tsp grated nutmeg

2.5ml/½ tsp salt

1.5ml/¼ tsp black pepper

4 eggs

3 hard-boiled eggs

For the pastry:

500g/1¼lb self-raising (self-rising) flour

5ml/1 tsp salt

130g/4½oz margarine

75ml/5 tbsp water

1 egg yolk, lightly beaten

Energy 274kcal/1138kJ; Protein 9g; Carbohydrate 11g, of which sugars 1.7g; Fat 21.9g, of which saturates 13.4g; Cholesterol 95mg; Calcium 83mg; Fibre 0.6g; Sodium 131mg

Andean spiced potatoes
Ajiaco de papas

An ajiaco is a stew from the Andes that gets its name from aji, a generic word for hot pepper. The dish combines potatoes, fresh cheese and chilli: there are many variations but these three main ingredients are always included. It can be served with rice and vegetables, or with roasted or grilled meats.

1 Boil the potatoes in their skins in lightly salted water for 20 minutes, until tender. Peel them and crush lightly (they do not need to be mashed to a purée). Set aside.

2 Heat the oil in a frying pan over medium heat and fry the spring onions and garlic for about 8 minutes, until browned.

3 Add the chilli sauce and paprika, season with salt and pepper, then stir in the potatoes, milk and water.

4 Mash the cheese with a fork and add to the potato mixture with the chopped eggs. Stir with a wooden spoon and leave to simmer for 5 minutes before serving.

Serves 6

1kg/2¼lb floury potatoes, such as King Edward

60ml/4 tbsp vegetable oil

6 spring onions (scallions), chopped

5ml/1 tsp grated garlic

30ml/2 tbsp chilli sauce

5ml/1 tsp paprika

250ml/8fl oz/1 cup evaporated milk

120ml/4fl oz/½ cup water

150g/5oz feta cheese

4 hard-boiled eggs, roughly chopped

salt and ground black pepper

Energy 306kcal/1281kJ; Protein 11.6g; Carbohydrate 28.7g, of which sugars 2.8g; Fat 17.1g, of which saturates 5.5g; Cholesterol 144mg; Calcium 129mg; Fibre 1.8g; Sodium 427mg.

Fried beans with eggs and plantain
Tacu tacu

Serves 6

250ml/8fl oz/1 cup vegetable oil

1 large onion, finely diced

30ml/2 tbsp chilli sauce

1kg/2¼lb/4 cups haricot (navy) beans, cooked or canned

1kg/2¼lb/4 cups cooked white rice (see page 103)

6–12 eggs

2 plantains, peeled and sliced

salt

onion salsa (see page 26) and chilli salsa (see page 84), to serve

Beans are very popular in Peru and are eaten regularly. They feature in soups, stews, rice dishes like this one, and even desserts. It is said that tacu tacu, traditionally made with leftovers, has its origins in the kitchens of African slaves, but it also has similarities with the food of neighbouring countries. Tacu tacu is traditionally served with fried plantains (tajadas).

1 Heat 75ml/5 tbsp of the oil in a non-stick frying pan over medium heat and fry the onion for 10 minutes until browned.

2 Stir the chilli sauce into the onion, then add the cooked beans and rice. Increase the heat to high and stir-fry the mixture, turning with a spatula, until the rice is developing a golden crust. Remove from the heat and leave to stand for 2 minutes.

3 Heat the remaining oil in another pan and fry the plantain slices over medium-high heat for 3 minutes on each side, until golden. Drain and keep warm while you fry the eggs.

4 Scoop a portion of the tacu tacu shaped like an upturned boat on to each plate and top with the fried eggs. Accompany with the fried plantains and place some onion salsa and chilli salsa on the table.

Energy 777kcal/3267kJ; Protein 29.8g; Carbohydrate 101.2g, of which sugars 12.6g; Fat 31.2g, of which saturates 5.6g; Cholesterol 381mg; Calcium 228mg; Fibre 12.1g; Sodium 796mg.

Cassava stuffed with cheese
Yucas rellenas con queso

Serves 6

1.5kg/3¼lb cassava

1 egg

100g/3¾oz plain (all-purpose) flour

200g/7oz mild-flavoured, buttery cheese, such as Cheddar, or Edam, cut into 12 small pieces

250ml/8fl oz/1 cup vegetable oil

salt

boiled rice and onion or chilli salsa, to serve

Cassava originates from tropical America. It is said that the Maya first grew this tuberous plant for food, but it is much used by all the Amazonian tribes, who even brew an alcoholic beverage from it, called masato. There are around 160 varieties, adapted to different growing conditions. Cassava has been eaten in Peru for a long time, usually as an accompaniment but also in tasty recipes like this one.

1 Cut the ends off the cassava and chop it into 7.5cm/3in sections. Remove the peel by making a lengthways cut and opening the skin with a knife. Place the peeled cassava in a large pan with water to cover and 5ml/1 tsp salt. Bring to the boil and simmer, covered, for 25 minutes.

2 When the cassava is tender, drain it and mash it while still warm. Beat in the egg and season with 5ml/1 tsp salt. Spread the mash on to a tray or board to cool.

3 Cover your palm lightly in flour, spread some of the cassava mash on it, place a piece of cheese in the centre and close the mixture around it, sealing it well, to make an oval-shaped ball. Roll the ball in flour and place on a plate. Repeat to make 12 balls.

4 Heat the oil in a pan and fry the balls over high heat until golden, turning them carefully to avoid breaking. Don't crowd the pan: it is best to fry two at a time. Drain on kitchen paper and serve with rice and onion or chilli salsa.

Energy 548kcal/2299kJ; Protein 14.3g; Carbohydrate 66.2g, of which sugars 14.5g; Fat 26.7g, of which saturates 7.6g; Cholesterol 58mg; Calcium 345mg; Fibre 6.5g; Sodium 452mg.

Quinoa stew
Pesque de quinua

When the Spanish conquerors came to America they were looking for gold and silver, land and power. Today the minerals are depleted, but potato, corn, cassava, lucuma, quinoa and other plants remain. In Inca times quinoa was considered to be sacred, and the emperor would sow the first seeds of the season. It is important to wash the quinoa several times before using it, to remove any traces of saponine.

1 Place the quinoa in a pan with the water and bring to the boil over high heat, then reduce the heat and simmer, covered, for 20 minutes, until the water has been absorbed.

2 Slowly add the milk to the quinoa, stirring gently, then add the oil and the beaten eggs, still stirring.

3 Add the slices of cheese and the chilli sauce and season to taste. Cook for a further 2 minutes, stirring, then remove from the heat and serve hot, accompanied by a good tomato or onion salsa.

Cook's tip For the tomato salsa, combine chopped tomatoes with finely sliced spring onions (scallions), chopped chilli, lime juice, salt and oil. This dish is a good accompaniment to grilled steak, if the meal is not vegetarian, but because of quinoa's high protein content it makes a meal in itself.

Serves 4

250g/9oz/1½ cups quinoa, well washed in at least 3 changes of water

1 litre/1¾ pints/4 cups water

250ml/8fl oz/1 cup fresh full cream (whole) milk or evaporated milk

60ml/4 tbsp vegetable oil

2 eggs, beaten

250g/9oz feta cheese, sliced

5ml/1 tsp chilli sauce

salt and ground black pepper

tomato salsa (see Cook's tip), to serve

Energy 501kcal/2082kJ; Protein 21.3g; Carbohydrate 39.5g, of which sugars 7.4g; Fat 29.6g, of which saturates 12.1g; Cholesterol 149mg; Calcium 414mg; Fibre 0g; Sodium 1007mg.

Wheat and fresh cheese stew
Trigo guisado

Wheat arrived with the Spanish conquerors and was gradually adopted by the Peruvians. Wholegrain wheat, or mote, is sold husked and is often eaten as an accompaniment to guinea pig. Queso fresco can be substituted with a mild feta.

1 Wash the wheat in at least three changes of water, then soak it for 8 hours.

2 Drain the wheat and put it in a large pan. Add 2 litres/3½ pints/8 cups water. Bring to the boil and cook for 1 hour, checking from time to time that it does not dry out: add a little more water once or twice if necessary.

3 Add the potatoes to the wheat and cook for a further 20 minutes, until the potatoes and wheat are tender.

4 Stir in the cheese, milk and chopped parsley. Leave to simmer gently for 10 minutes, then remove from the heat and serve.

Serves 4

250g/9oz/1 cup wholegrain wheat (wheat berries)

2 medium King Edward potatoes, peeled and quartered

200g/7oz queso fresco or mild feta cheese, thinly sliced

250ml/8fl oz/1 cup full cream (whole) milk

45ml/3 tbsp chopped parsley

salt and ground black pepper

Energy 448kcal/1889kJ; Protein 16.4g; Carbohydrate 68.4g, of which sugars 5g; Fat 14g, of which saturates 8.4g; Cholesterol 44mg; Calcium 292mg; Fibre 1.3g; Sodium 768mg.

Peruvian white rice
Arroz blanco

Serves 4

250g/9oz/1¼ cups American long grain rice

45ml/3 tbsp vegetable oil

2 garlic cloves, chopped, crushed or sliced

300ml/½ pint/1¼ cups water

15ml/1 tbsp salt

When it first arrived with the Spanish, rice was a great luxury because in the early years the crop yields were so small. Rice with meat was a special dish confined to the tables of the wealthy, but gradually more was grown, and following the Chinese immigration of the 19th century it was embraced enthusiastically everywhere. Today it is a staple in Peru. This basic recipe produces the grainy texture Peruvians like.

1 Wash the rice four or five times in cold water, then leave to drain.

2 In a medium pan, heat the oil and fry the garlic for 2–3 minutes, or until it is golden. Add the water, salt and rice and bring to the boil. Simmer uncovered for 15 minutes, or until the water has been absorbed.

3 Stir once, then turn the heat to low, cover the pan and cook for a further 15 minutes.

Variations When the rice is almost cooked, add a small can of corn kernels, drained, or a handful of frozen peas. Add a handful of small dried Chinese prawns (shrimp) to the rice, if it is to accompany a fish dish.

Energy 301kcal/1254kJ; Protein 4.8g; Carbohydrate 50.3g, of which sugars 0.1g; Fat 8.6g, of which saturates 0.9g; Cholesterol 0mg; Calcium 13mg; Fibre 0.1g; Sodium 491mg.

Dried peas
Alverjitas secas

Serves 4

250g/9oz/1¼ cups dried peas, soaked for 8 hours, and drained

1.5 litres/2½ pints/6¼ cups water

75ml/5 tbsp olive oil

1 medium onion, finely diced

1 small tomato, chopped

salt

white rice (see page 103) and onion salsa (see page 26), to serve

Dried beans, peas and lentils are part of the staple diet all over America. Many Peruvian dishes are enriched by the addition of ingredients such as onions fried in oil, and all beans are excellent treated in this way, whichever variety you use – the only difference will be in the cooking times. Using the best olive oil makes these particularly delicious. This dish is a meal in itself, or can accompany any meat dish.

1 Place the peas in a large pan with the water and bring to the boil, then reduce the heat and simmer, covered, for 1 hour, until soft. Stir from time to time to prevent them sticking. If they start to dry out, add a little extra boiling water from the kettle, but not too much at a time.

2 Heat the oil in a frying pan and fry the onions over medium heat for about 10 minutes, until browned. Add the tomato and cook for a further 5 minutes.

3 Pour the onion and tomato mixture, together with all the oil, over the peas and stir it in. Season to taste and leave for 15 minutes for the flavours to infuse before serving with rice and onion salsa.

Variation To make a richer dish, try adding some chopped smoked bacon or sausage for extra flavour. Peruvians often add a piece of pork skin to the pot while boiling dried beans to make them softer.

Energy 331kcal/1388kJ; Protein 15.2g; Carbohydrate 36.9g, of which sugars 2.9g; Fat 14.6g, of which saturates 2.1g; Cholesterol 0mg; Calcium 37mg; Fibre 3.4g; Sodium 25mg.

Squash, potato and corn stew
Locro de zapallo

A locro is a kind of stew from the south of Peru (it is also found in Argentina, where fruits are added). There is a very large yellow squash in Peru, so big that it is carved up into pieces and sold by the kilogram in the markets. Called zapallo, it is soft and buttery and is used in many recipes, from soups to puddings. Butternut squash has been substituted here, and gives a delicious nutty flavour.

1 Heat the oil in a large pan over medium heat and fry the onion and garlic for 10 minutes, until the onion is browned. Add the tomato, and cook for another 5 minutes.

2 Add the pieces of squash, corn on the cob and potatoes to the pan and pour in the water. Season with salt, bring to the boil and cook over medium heat for 20 minutes, covered, until the potatoes are tender.

3 Remove the pan from the heat and crumble the cheese over the vegetables. Serve immediately, accompanied by rice.

Cook's tip To prepare the butternut squash it is best to peel it first. The skin is thin, and comes off easily with a vegetable peeler. When peeled, remove the top and bottom and chop it in half lengthways, remove the seeds and filaments and cut into chunks.

Serves 6

75ml/5 tbsp vegetable oil

1 small onion, finely chopped

2 garlic cloves, finely sliced or chopped

1 medium tomato, chopped

1 butternut squash, weighing approximately 1kg/2¼lb, peeled and cut into 2.5cm/1in chunks

3 corn on the cob, cut into 2.5cm/1in chunks

1 kg/2¼lb white potatoes, peeled and quartered

500ml/17fl oz/generous 2 cups water

100g/3¾oz feta cheese

salt

white rice (see page 103), to serve

Energy 329kcal/1382kJ; Protein 8.3g; Carbohydrate 45.2g, of which sugars 11g; Fat 14g, of which saturates 3.7g; Cholesterol 12mg; Calcium 124mg; Fibre 4.3g; Sodium 395mg.

Sweet potato purée
Puré de camotes

The sweet potato probably originated in Central America. It is much used in Peru, where it is usually served boiled with savoury dishes such as cebiche or escabeche, or baked for a sweeter result. Fried sweet potato is indispensable for a good chicharrones sandwich, its natural sweet flavour is also delicious in desserts. This purée is an excellent accompaniment for roasted meats such as pork or turkey.

1 Put the sweet potatoes in a large pan with enough water to cover and boil them in their skins for 30 minutes, covered, until tender. Drain and peel them as soon as they are cool enough to handle.

2 Mash the peeled sweet potatoes and return them to the pan. Stir in the butter and sugar and cook gently for about 8 minutes, stirring constantly to avoid the mixture sticking.

3 Off the heat, stir the orange juice into the purée and serve immediately, topped with extra butter, if you wish.

Variation For an extra-sweet version of this recipe, pour the purée into an ovenproof dish and dot the top with marshmallows. Bake for 20–30 minutes in a moderate oven until the purée is heated through and the marshmallows are melting and golden.

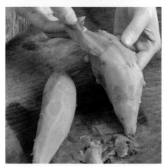

Serves 8

1kg/2¼lb yellow sweet
  potatoes, preferably South
  American

15ml/1 tbsp butter

75ml/5 tbsp caster
  (superfine) sugar

juice of 1 orange

Energy 162kcal/689kJ; Protein 1.6g; Carbohydrate 37g, of which sugars 17.5g; Fat 1.9g, of which saturates 1.1g; Cholesterol 4mg; Calcium 36mg; Fibre 3g; Sodium 65mg.

Fried and baked plantains
Chifles, patacones, tajadas y demas

Chifles: Makes about 30

120ml/4fl oz/½ cup vegetable oil

1 green plantain, thinly sliced

salt

Patacones: Makes about 15

250ml/8fl oz/1 cup vegetable oil

1 green plantain, cut into 1cm/½in slices

salt

Baked plantain: Serves 2

1 ripe plantain, peeled

The plantain is related to the banana, but has to be cooked before it can be eaten. It is believed to have reached America with black African slaves. Chifles make an irresistible snack when freshly made; patacones are popular as a side dish, after the initial frying the slices are flattened before being fried again; and baked plantain makes a very good accompaniment for roasted meat, especially pork and turkey.

1 To make chifles: Heat the oil in a frying pan over medium-high heat. Drop in the plantain slices and fry until they are golden, sprinkling with salt as they cook. Lift out the chips using a slotted spoon and drain thoroughly.

2 To make patacones: Heat the oil in a frying pan over medium-high meat and fry the plantain slices for about 4 minutes on each side, until they are golden. Lift them out using a slotted spoon and drain on kitchen paper.

3 Put the patacones on a board or in a press and flatten them without breaking them. You need to press firmly rather than bang them flat. Return the patacones to the frying pan and fry them again for 3 minutes on each side until they are golden and crisp. Drain thoroughly and season with plenty of salt.

4 For baked plantain: Heat the oven to 200°C/400°F/Gas 6. Put the plantain in an oiled roasting pan and bake for 30 minutes.

Energy 28kcal/115kJ; Protein 0.1g; Carbohydrate 2g, of which sugars 0.4g; Fat 2.2g, of which saturates 0.2g; Cholesterol 0mg; Calcium 1mg; Fibre 0.1g; Sodium 0mg.

Desserts, cakes and cookies

Desserts in Peruvian cooking are often based on milk, fruit or rice, and sometimes all three. Sweet, milky puddings are particular favourites.

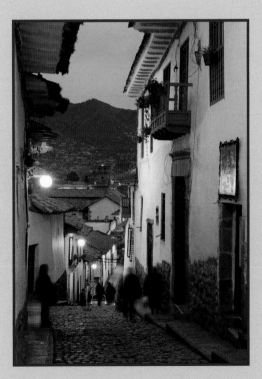

A delightful tradition of sweet treats

The only sweet foods known in the Inca empire were fruits and honey. These were considered delicacies and were eaten alongside savoury dishes. There is no question that the Incas valued sweet flavours, as they learned to dry tubers in the sun to increase their sweetness. They would probably have eaten native plants such as the sugary root called macon, which can be consumed raw like a fruit, and the South American sweet potato. But there is little available evidence: just the remnants of pottery from Inca times decorated with fruits, and the culinary traditions of a few native communities that have survived.

The Spanish colonists brought sugar cane (which was introduced to Spain by the Arabs) and initiated Peruvians into its many uses. They also brought recipes for sweet dishes with Spanish ingredients and developed and improved others using Peru's native fruits. An important innovation was the introduction of ovens for baking bread and cakes, which was unheard of before the 16th century. Other Spanish methods, such as the use of eggs and flour to thicken dishes, and cooking with milk, further extended the range of Peruvian sweet dishes.

Dishes such as manjarblanco became popular during the Spanish viceroyalty. The original recipe, like that of blancmange, included chicken, and at one time potato was used as a base, creating a distinctive Peruvian version, but today it is made only with milk and sugar and resembles dulce de leche, a favourite in Argentina and Paraguay.

Once life became more stable, cooks developed their skills, and bakers and sweet makers became part of Peruvian life, building up the country's repertoire of cakes. This wealth of classic recipes is best preserved today in the cloistered kitchens of the country's convents, where the nuns still keep treasured recipe books that date back to their founding years.

Purple corn pudding
Mazamorra morada

This confection of corn and dried fruits, thickened with sweet potato starch, is quintessentially Peruvian. Traditionally fed to children to give them energy, there are many variations on the recipe, using ingredients such as squash, flour and molasses, quinoa or tapioca. All are sweet, healthy and gentle on the stomach.

1 Place the sachet of corn powder in a large pan with the apple, cinnamon stick, cloves and orange peel. Stir in the water and bring to the boil. Simmer for 30 minutes over medium heat.

2 Strain the mixture and return the liquid to the pan. Add the dried fruits and simmer for a further 30 minutes, then stir in the sugar.

3 Blend the potato flour with 100ml/3½fl oz/scant ½ cup water and add it to the pan, stir for 5 minutes until the mixture thickens, then remove from the heat.

4 Pour into a serving bowl, or into individual bowls (distributing the fruit evenly). Sprinkle with cinnamon and leave to cool before serving.

Serves 6

1 sachet purple corn powder

1 apple, roughly chopped

1 cinnamon stick

3 cloves

1 small piece (2cm/¾in) dried orange peel

1½ litres/2½ pints/6¼ cups water

50g/2oz prunes

50g/2oz dried apricots

50g/2oz dried peaches

50g/2oz dried pears

90ml/6 tbsp sugar

45ml/3 tbsp potato flour (starch)

ground cinnamon, for sprinkling

Energy 122kcal/518kJ; Protein 1.8g; Carbohydrate 29.4g, of which sugars 23.4g; Fat 0.3g, of which saturates 0g; Cholesterol 0mg; Calcium 29mg; Fibre 2.4g; Sodium 6mg.

Spiced rice pudding
Arroz zambito

Serves 6

250g/9oz/1¼ cups rice

1 litre/1¾ pints/4 cups water

3 cinnamon sticks

3 cloves

250g/9oz/1¼ cups soft dark brown sugar

45ml/3 tbsp desiccated (dry unsweetened shredded) coconut

100g/3¾oz/⅔ cup raisins

45ml/3 tbsp chopped walnuts

350ml/12fl oz evaporated milk

ground cinnamon, to dust

In a culture in which rice is eaten every day it would be impossible not to have some desserts made with it, and Peru has several favourites. Milk pudding made with rice is a popular dish in many other countries, but the spices, fruits and dark brown sugar in this Peruvian version make it different and delicious.

1 Wash the rice. Put the water in a large heavy pan with the cinnamon sticks, cloves and sugar and bring to the boil.

2 Add the rice and the coconut. Cook over a medium-high heat, stirring often, for 20–25 minutes or until the rice is cooked.

3 Add the raisins, walnuts and evaporated milk, and simmer for 10 minutes, stirring from time to time.

4 Spoon into individual dishes and leave to cool. Dust with cinnamon before serving.

Energy 518kcal/2181kJ; Protein 9.7g; Carbohydrate 95.1g, of which sugars 61.8g; Fat 12.5g, of which saturates 5.9g; Cholesterol 10mg; Calcium 198mg; Fibre 1.6g; Sodium 82mg.

Almond cream
Bienmesabe

There was a time when families were large, with several generations living together, and many hungry children to feed. Home cooks would work all day to produce appetizers, soups, main dishes, desserts and sweets. From that time comes this recipe, with a name that describes the experience of taking a spoonful of it – bienmesabe means "it tastes good to me," and this really does taste good. The egg yolks and nuts give it a luxurious richness, ideal for a luxurious dinner party dessert.

1 In a small bowl mix the cornflour to a smooth paste with a little of the milk and set aside. Pour the remaining milk into a heavy pan and add the cinnamon stick.

2 Bring to the boil, then reduce the heat and stir in the slaked cornflour using a wooden spoon. Keep stirring until it boils and thickens, then add the sugar.

3 When the sugar has dissolved, add the coconut, almonds and walnuts to the pan and boil for 10 minutes over medium heat, stirring the pudding constantly.

4 Remove the pan from the heat and gradually add the beaten egg yolks until thoroughly mixed in.

5 Return the pan to the heat and cook the mixture for a further 10 minutes, still stirring constantly, until it is very thick: when stirring with the spoon it should be possible to see the bottom of the pan.

6 Pour into individual serving bowls and leave to cool. Decorate with a sprinkling of nuts before serving.

Cook's Tip To toast the almonds for decoration, spread them in one layer on a baking tray and place in a hot oven for a few minutes. Check them carefully as they scorch very quickly. You can also toast them under the grill (broiler), but again you will need to watch them constantly to avoid burning.

Serves 6

15ml/1 tbsp cornflour (cornstarch)

500ml/17fl oz/generous 2 cups milk

1 small cinnamon stick

125g/4¼oz/scant ¾ cup caster (superfine) sugar

75ml/5 tbsp desiccated (dry unsweetened shredded) coconut

75ml/5 tbsp ground almonds

75ml/5 tbsp ground walnuts

3 egg yolks, very well beaten

flaked (sliced) almonds and walnut halves, to decorate

Energy 426kcal/1779kJ; Protein 12.7g; Carbohydrate 33.2g, of which sugars 30.2g; Fat 27.9g, of which saturates 10.1g; Cholesterol 110mg; Calcium 257mg; Fibre 3.7g; Sodium 81mg.

Sigh of a Lima woman
Suspiro de Limeña

The women of Lima have always been famed for their wit and beauty, and the story goes that after tasting this dessert a 19th-century poet commented, "It is like the sigh of a lady from Lima." There was no more to say: the sweet was described and named all in one. Once more, milk, eggs and sugar make a wonderful combination, but the basis of this pudding is dulce de leche, the sweet fudge sauce made from reduced condensed milk, which is adored by all South Americans. Suspiro de Limeña is extremely rich, so it's best served in small portions.

Serves 6

350ml/12fl oz/1¼ cups sweetened condensed milk

350ml/12fl oz/1½ cups evaporated milk

5 egg yolks

5ml/1 tsp vanilla extract

250g/9oz/1¼ cups caster (superfine) sugar

250ml/8fl oz white port or white vermouth

3 egg whites

ground cinnamon, to dust

1 To make the dulce de leche, on which this recipe is based, mix the condensed and evaporated milks together in a pan.

2 Bring slowly to the boil and then cook over medium heat for 40 minutes, stirring constantly to prevent burning, until reduced and thick. The colour should have changed from cream to a light toffee colour. Remove from the heat and leave to cool a little.

3 When the dulce de leche has cooled slightly, but is still warm, add the egg yolks and vanilla to the mixture and stir thoroughly. Pour into individual serving dishes and leave to cool.

4 To make the topping, combine the sugar with the port or vermouth in a small pan. Heat gently, stirring, until the sugar has dissolved, then bring to the boil and cook the syrup over a high heat for 7 minutes.

5 Meanwhile, whisk the egg whites until they form stiff peaks. Still whisking, pour the hot syrup into the whites and continue to whisk until the meringue is cool and thick.

6 Pile the meringue on top of the caramel mixture, dust with cinnamon and serve.

Energy 308kcal/1292kJ; Protein 11.9g; Carbohydrate 38.4g, of which sugars 38.4g; Fat 12.9g, of which saturates 6.4g; Cholesterol 199mg; Calcium 340mg; Fibre 0g; Sodium 156mg.

Bread pudding with cherry syrup
Budín de pan

Serves 10

1 small loaf of white bread (12 slices) or 6 bread rolls, reduced to crumbs

2 x 350ml/12fl oz cans evaporated milk

60ml/4 tbsp caster (superfine) sugar

3 eggs, lightly beaten

15ml/1 tbsp butter, melted, plus extra for greasing

5ml/1 tsp ground cinnamon

30ml/2 tbsp port

pinch of salt

150g/5oz/1 cup raisins, tossed in flour

For the cherry syrup:

250g/9oz/1¼ cups dried cherries

250g/9oz/1¼ cups caster (superfine) sugar

500ml/17fl oz/generous 2 cups water

Bakeries prepare large trays of this pudding ready for the afternoon when children get home from school. It has long been considered especially suitable for the young, because it is gentle on the stomach. Some bakers make a deluxe version using 'Chancay' rolls, which are made with egg-enriched dough.

1 Preheat the oven to 160°C/325°F/Gas 3 and grease a 25cm/10in diameter cake tin (pan). Put the breadcrumbs in a mixing bowl with the milk and soak for 5–10 minutes.

2 Add the sugar, eggs, butter, cinnamon, port and salt. Mix everything together thoroughly, then lightly stir in the raisins.

3 Pour the mixture into the prepared tin and bake for 40 minutes, or until a skewer pushed into the middle comes out clean. Leave to cool.

4 To make the syrup, place the cherries in a small pan with the sugar and water.

5 Heat gently, stirring, until the sugar has dissolved, then bring to the boil and simmer for 15 minutes until syrupy. Leave to cool.

6 When the pudding is cold, run a knife or spatula around the sides and turn it out on to a plate, removing the tin slowly. Serve in slices with the syrup poured over.

Energy 300kcal/1269kJ; Protein 11.3g; Carbohydrate 51.4g, of which sugars 32.7g; Fat 6.6g, of which saturates 3.2g; Cholesterol 72mg; Calcium 251mg; Fibre 1.1g; Sodium 333mg.

Bean purée
Frejol colado

Driving south from Lima, after about 160km/100 miles you will see street vendors at petrol stations or in town squares selling dried pumpkin shells. These are not empty, but full of the most representative sweet of the province of Chincha: frejol colado. Flavoured with sesame seeds and with just the right degree of sweetness, it is a treat that every visitor wants to take back home.

1 Boil the beans in the water for 1 hour, or until tender. If using kidney beans, boil rapidly for 15 minutes to destroy toxins. Drain and cool the beans, then peel off the outer skins.

2 Put the beans into a blender or food processor with the evaporated milk and blend together until smooth.

3 Pour the mixture into a pan and add the sugar, cinnamon stick and cloves. Cook over a medium heat, stirring frequently with a wooden spoon, for 25–30 minutes, until thick. Cool.

4 Spoon the frejol colado into individual serving bowls and refrigerate. When ready to serve sprinkle the toasted sesame seeds on top.

Serves 6

250g/9oz/1¼ cups red kidney beans, butter (lima) beans, soaked for 12 hours and drained

2 litres/3½ pints/8 cups water

250ml/8fl oz/1 cup evaporated milk

250g/9oz/1¼ cups caster (superfine) sugar

1 cinnamon stick

2 or 3 cloves

30ml/2 tbsp toasted sesame seeds

Energy 350kcal/1483kJ; Protein 13.6g; Carbohydrate 66.3g, of which sugars 48.9g; Fat 5.2g, of which saturates 1.5g; Cholesterol 7mg; Calcium 206mg; Fibre 6.9g; Sodium 59mg.

Spiced syrup cake
Huevo chimbo

This is a sweet and very indulgent cake, enriched with a total of 12 egg yolks. It is made deliciously moist by the unusual method of simmering the baked slices in a spicy sugar syrup, after it has been baked.

1 Preheat the oven to 160°C/325°F/Gas 3 and grease or line a 25cm/10in square cake tin (pan).

2 Whisk the egg yolks in a bowl until they are thick and almost white. Sift in the flour and baking powder and fold in gently.

3 Pour the mixture into the prepared tin and bake for 20 minutes, until springy and golden. Remove from the oven. Leave to cool in the tin.

4 Put the water, sugar, cinnamon and cloves in a wide pan. Heat gently, stirring, until the sugar has dissolved, then boil the mixture for 10 minutes over a high heat to make a syrup. Reduce the heat to low.

5 Cut the cake into slices about 6 x 3cm/2½ x 1¼in and slide them gently into the syrup. Simmer for 10 minutes, then lift them out with a slotted spoon and leave to cool. Decorate with toasted, flaked almonds.

Serves 8

12 egg yolks

15ml/1 tbsp self-raising (self-rising) flour

5ml/1 tsp baking powder

1 litre/1¾ pints/4 cups water

500g/1¼lb/2½ cups sugar

1 large cinnamon stick

3 cloves

flaked (sliced) almonds, toasted, to decorate

Energy 344kcal/1456kJ; Protein 4.8g; Carbohydrate 66.8g, of which sugars 65.3g; Fat 8.3g, of which saturates 2.4g; Cholesterol 302mg; Calcium 71mg; Fibre 0.1g; Sodium 17mg.

Wedding biscuits
Empanaditas de boda

Makes 15

250g/9oz/2¼ cups self-raising (self-rising) flour

10ml/2 tsp baking powder

250g/9oz/1¼ cups caster (superfine) sugar

250g/9oz/generous 1 cup lard

30ml/2 tbsp water

1 egg yolk

45ml/3 tbsp milk

50g/2oz/¼ cup toasted sesame seeds

In some towns in the North Central region these biscuits are sold at local festivals. They are known as 'wedding biscuits' because they are most often made for such celebrations, but street vendors also sell them, freshly made, warm and delicious.

1 Preheat the oven to 200°C/400°F/Gas 6 and grease a large baking sheet.

2 Sift the flour with the baking powder and stir in the sugar. Make a well in the centre and add the lard, cut into small pieces, and the water. Gradually rub the lard and water in to the dry ingredients, adding a little more water if needed, and knead the mixture for about 10 minutes to form a smooth dough.

3 Form the dough into a roll about 7.5cm/3in in diameter and cut it into 1cm/½in slices.

4 Lay the slices on the baking sheet, spacing them well.

5 Beat the egg yolk lightly with the milk and brush the top of each biscuit with the mixture. Sprinkle with the sesame seeds and bake for 20 minutes, until they are golden brown. Leave them on the baking sheet to cool.

Cook's tip You can make tiny biscuits for parties by rolling a smaller dough roll and slicing thinner rounds. The baking time for smaller biscuits will need to be reduced.

Energy 295kcal/1230kJ; Protein 2.5g; Carbohydrate 30.2g, of which sugars 17.8g; Fat 19.1g, of which saturates 7.2g; Cholesterol 29mg; Calcium 95mg; Fibre 0.8g; Sodium 64mg.

Caramel-filled cookies
Alfajores

These cookies are a classic Peruvian treat. They are really popular, and every bakery, delicatessen, and sweet shop has its own version of the recipe. Even individual families have their own particular recipes. The cookies are made in all sizes – some as large as a plate – and filled with different kinds of manjar blanco, the Peruvian name for dulce de leche. Alfajores are eaten with great enjoyment all along the coast of Peru.

Makes 10–12

250g/9oz/2¼ cups self-raising (self-rising) flour, plus extra for dusting

250g/9oz/2¼ cups cornflour (cornstarch)

50g/2oz/½ cup icing (confectioners') sugar

100g/3¾oz/scant ½ cup margarine

1 egg yolk

15ml/1 tbsp milk

400g/14oz can dulce de leche or sweetened condensed milk (see Cook's tips)

1 Preheat the oven to 160°C/325°F/Gas 3. Grease a large baking sheet, and line with baking parchment.

2 Sift the flour, cornflour and 45ml/3 tbsp of the icing sugar into a mixing bowl and rub in the margarine. When the margarine is incorporated, add the egg yolk and milk, kneading the ingredients lightly but thoroughly to form a soft dough.

3 Dust a work surface with flour and roll out the dough to about 4mm/⅙in thick. Cut out circles using a 4cm/1½in plain cookie cutter and lay them on the prepared baking sheet, leaving space for them to spread.

4 Prick each cookie in two places with a fork, place in the oven and bake for 20 minutes, or until golden.

5 Remove from the oven and transfer to a wire tray. Leave the cookies until they are completely cool.

6 Sandwich pairs of the cookies together with dulce de leche, and arrange on a plate. Sift the remaining icing sugar over the filled cookies.

Cook's tip To make manjar blanco, or dulce de leche, from condensed milk, remove the paper wrapping, and place the can in a pan with water to come to 1in/2cm from the top. Bring the water to the boil, reduce to a simmer, cover, and leave bubbling for 2–3 hours, topping up with boiling water as necessary. Don't let the water stop simmering, otherwise the milk won't thicken, and don't let the water dry up, otherwise the can will explode. Leave the can to cool before opening it.

For a softer dulce de leche, you need only boil it for 1½–2 hours, but a firmer texture is needed for these cookies.

Variation To make cocktail-sized alfajores, roll the dough very thinly (no more than 2mm/¹⁄₁₂in thick) and cut out using a 2cm/¾in cutter. They will take 10–15 minutes to bake. Serve the dulche de leche on the side as a dip.

Energy 337kcal/1423kJ; Protein 5.1g; Carbohydrate 57.9g, of which sugars 23.3g; Fat 11g, of which saturates 2.3g; Cholesterol 29mg; Calcium 179mg; Fibre 0.7g; Sodium 201mg.

Chicken neck pastries
Guarguero

Many Peruvian sweets have amusing or charming names that describe their appearance, such as 'little handkerchiefs' and 'flying saucers' and these delicious caramel-filled fried pastries are called 'chicken necks'. They are sold in bakeries and at street stalls. Crisp and light, they can be served as a dessert or as a snack with a cup of tea or coffee.

1 Sift the flour and baking powder into a bowl, make a well in the centre and add the egg yolks and margarine.

2 Mix the flour, egg and margarine together, gradually adding the pisco or grappa. Knead the dough until smooth, then cover and leave to rest for 1 hour.

3 Dust the work surface with flour and roll the dough out very thinly (about 2mm/¹⁄₁₆in). Cut the dough into small triangles about 7.5cm/3in across.

4 Heat the oil in a frying pan. When it is hot, start rolling up the triangles into cylinders, beginning at a long side and securing the apex with a little egg white. Work quickly, and drop each cylinder into the pan as soon as it is formed so that it keeps its shape.

5 Fry the pastries over a medium heat for about 3 minutes, turning them carefully, until they are crisp and golden.

6 As the pastries are done, remove them from the pan with a slotted spoon and drain on kitchen paper. Leave to cool completely.

7 Fill the pastries with dulce de leche, spooning or piping it from both ends, and dust them with sifted icing sugar before serving. If not serving immediately, keep in an airtight container, then fill and dust just before serving.

Makes 16

30ml/2 tbsp self-raising (self-rising) flour, plus extra for dusting

5ml/1 tsp baking powder

2 egg yolks

50g/2oz/¹⁄₄ cup margarine

30ml/2 tbsp pisco or grappa

vegetable oil, for frying

1 egg white, lightly beaten

400g/14oz can dulce de leche or sweetened condensed milk (see Cook's tip on p123)

45ml/3 tbsp icing (confectioners') sugar for dusting

Energy 169kcal/708kJ; Protein 2.9g; Carbohydrate 18.3g, of which sugars 16.8g; Fat 9.5g, of which saturates 2.4g; Cholesterol 34mg; Calcium 80mg; Fibre 0.1g; Sodium 40mg.

Useful addresses

Australia

Incas Restaurant
Peruvian restaurant
92 Enmore Road
Newtown, Sydney 2042
Tel: +61 02 9550 4709
www.incasrestaurant.com.au

Mi Peru
Peruvian food store
Mitchell Road, PO Box 943
Brookvale DC 2100
Tel: +61 04 1843 5546

Canada

El Fogón
Peruvian restaurant
543 St Clair Ave West
Toronto, Canada
Tel: +1 416 850 8041
www.elfogon.ca

Maria's Brasa Chicken
Peruvian restaurant and
online supplier of yellow chilli
and chicha morada
117 Cross Avenue,
Oakville, Toronto
Tel: (905)582 9990
www.mariasbrasachicken.
com

United Kingdom

Anglo-Peruvian Trading Company
Peruvian food and drinks
25–27 Clarendon Road
London N8 0DD
Tel: +44 20 8889 8895
www.anglo-peruvian.com

El Aguajal
Peruvian restaurant
578 Kingsland Road
London E8 4AH
Tel: +44 20 7923 4883
www.elaguajal.co.uk

Mi Peru
Catering service specializing
in Peruvian food, and supplier
of pisco
Tel: +44 20 8960 3866
www.miperu.co.uk

Flor Arcaya de Deliot
Online supplier of purple corn
and speciality teas,
www.peruviancocatea.com

Latinland
Online supplies of Peruvian
ingredients
www.latinland.uk.com

United States

Amigofoods.com
Online store selling Peruvian
foods
Tel: +1 (800) 6272544
www.amigofoods.com

Andina Restaurant
Peruvian restaurant
1314 NW Glisan Street
Portland, Oregon 97209
Tel: +1 (503) 228 9535
www.andinarestaurant.com

Bedicomsa
Supplier of Peruvian grains
and beans

7461 SW 56 Street
Miami, Florida 33155
Tel: +1 (305) 984 4822
www.bedicomsa.com

Incafe
Suppliers of Peruvian coffee
12 Strathmore Rd
Brookline
Massachusetts 02445
Tel: +1 (617) 277 5986
www.incafeworld.com

Perusupermarket
Online supermarket
www.perusupermarket.com

Index